LONDON'S HISTORIC RAILWAY TERMINAL STATIONS

AN ILLUSTRATED HISTORY

LONDON'S HISTORIC RAILWAY TERMINAL STATIONS
AN ILLUSTRATED HISTORY

Geoff Swaine

PEN & SWORD
TRANSPORT

AN IMPRINT OF PEN & SWORD BOOKS LTD.
YORKSHIRE – PHILADELPHIA

First published in Great Britain in 2021 by
Pen and Sword Transport
An imprint of
Pen & Sword Books Ltd.
Yorkshire - Philadelphia

Copyright © Geoff Swaine, 2021

ISBN 978 1 52676 188 0

The right of Geoff Swaine to be identified as author of this work has been asserted by him in accordance with the Copyright, Designs and Patents Act 1988.

A CIP catalogue record for this book is available from the British Library.

Typeset by SJmagic DESIGN SERVICES, India.
Printed and bound by Printworks Global Ltd, London / Hong Kong.

Pen & Sword Books Ltd incorporates the imprints of Pen & Sword Books Archaeology, Atlas, Aviation, Battleground, Discovery, Family History, History, Maritime, Military, Naval, Politics, Railways, Select, Transport, True Crime, Fiction, Frontline Books, Leo Cooper, Praetorian Press, Seaforth Publishing, Wharncliffe and White Owl.

For a complete list of Pen & Sword titles please contact

PEN & SWORD BOOKS LIMITED
47 Church Street, Barnsley, South Yorkshire, S70 2AS, England
E-mail: enquiries@pen-and-sword.co.uk
Website: www.pen-and-sword.co.uk

or

PEN AND SWORD BOOKS
1950 Lawrence Rd, Havertown, PA 19083, USA
E-mail: Uspen-and-sword@casematepublishers.com
Website: www.penandswordbooks.com

CONTENTS

INTRODUCTION

The Rainhill trials of 1829 started it all off. For the first time people could travel by rail. It had been clearly seen and advertised that goods moved on rails would transform lives. Materials such as coal, milk, farming produce etc. could be brought right into the heart of a town or city in no time at all. The Liverpool to Manchester line was built to transport cotton bales from the docks of Liverpool to the mills of Manchester; an operation which previously may have taken four days by canal, now could be achieved in one. It became the first section of railway in the world to link two towns.

Railways were conceived and developed to move goods, because at the time the only practical way of moving items was by coast or canal. Using a road with a horse and cart was a non-starter except for very local work. The movement of products into areas of population immediately improved people's circumstances, providing a healthier and improved lifestyle. Being able to travel themselves on the railway enhanced those lives even more.

It was a double whammy which led to lines linking one town to the next in rapid succession. Entrepreneurs built a railway where they wanted it, and could see a profit. Often these lines were duplicated. As the 1830s progressed lines began to be linked to others which started a trend towards a network. Governments saw this and passed bills through Parliament for new lines without any wider consideration of the consequences. The country was in a slump and the expansion of the railways was bringing it into a new age of prosperity. People also saw that for the first time they could get to a market town and back within one day, improving their lives dramatically.

London was the capital city, a huge sprawl of mostly hovels where residents tried to eek out a living in any way they could. Virtually all of their food would have been sourced locally. Sometimes a pig or a cow was kept in a back yard. To connect a railway line to the capital became a priority. The government of the time knew this and gave it such priority, for it was giving the voters what they wanted.

Routes were planned from the north, but a stipulation determined by statute that no trains could come into the capital beyond the Euston and Marylebone Roads. To the south the first line to get close to the city centre was the London & Greenwich Railway (L&GR). To be a practical proposition this had to be elevated and built on brick arches – over 800 of them. The railway arriving at London Bridge was such a success that the L&GR increased the width so that the tracks could be rented to their rivals. The use of brick arches became the method by which many lines overcame the problem of crossing roads. The arches themselves were then rented to small businesses, for which, with modification, they were ideal premises, again showing how the coming of the railways improved prosperity.

By the 1850s the great long-distance railways had become established. All those little railways which often just went from one town to the next got swept up with amalgamations and sell-outs. The big railway companies ran long-distance excursions which became regular and popular. So great an impact did this have that day excursions at low cost were still being offered a century later.

There was one more thing that big companies desired at this point; a grand cathedral-like terminus station at the end of the line to firmly make a statement of their greatness. Don't forget that this was still the age before the motor car. Trains could travel at over 40mph on their beautiful, even track, where the poor old horse and carriage struggled to get close to 10mph on roads which in winter could sometimes become impassable. The transportation of goods was as important as passenger travel, quite possibly more so. So at every major London terminus there were adjacent goods yards.

In 1851, the Great Exhibition, for which a glass palace was built to house everything beneath it which was great about Britain, opened at Hyde Park in London. The railway companies reacted and offered one-day excursions from all parts of the country. It is thought that some 4 million people used these services to attend the event.

Brunel's Great Western Railway (GWR) opened completely between London and Bristol in 1841. It had a very gentle rise between London and Swindon and then fell slightly from Swindon to Bristol. Brunel sought to make it as level as he possibly could, with the whole route becoming known as 'Brunel's billiard table'. In the 1850s the magnificent Paddington Station appeared. Like most stations there was an original station built just beyond the site of the one we know today. Once the new structure was finished the lines were just diverted accordingly.

This book provides an insight into how all these magnificent buildings and sites developed. Unlike cathedrals, where the same layout stayed pretty much the same for centuries, stations had to keep pace with ever-improving technology. Increases in passenger usage ensured continuous thoughts of expansion and greater efficiencies. The service requirements of getting passengers to and from stations are always changing and passenger flows change to suit the comings and goings of buses, taxis and Underground trains.

The trains themselves will not be ignored here: they were the showpieces, crossing the country in all directions. The races to the North in the 1930s caused huge interest and generated large amounts of publicity. This was followed by World War II, in which the railways played a vital part.

In the early part of the twenty-first century, great investment has been put into the improvement and modernisation of the railways. It is from this point that we can take a mostly pictorial look at what we have and relish those hugely fascinating and interesting histories.

King's Cross was designed by Lewis Cubitt and opened in 1852 to serve the east coast rail route to Scotland. The design clearly shows the function of the building, with a generous forecourt for passengers and the public to appreciate. However, four generations of people have been deprived of this facility owing to the space being occupied by shops and other business concessions. Now thankfully it has all been removed for us to appreciate.

Above: The Lawn at Paddington Station has not seen a blade of grass in more than 150 years. But somehow these names don't get lost. This area was upgraded in 1933, which included the new end screen in the style of Wyatt (Brunel's architect for decoration and ornamentation).

Opposite above: Paddington was the pride of the GWR. Designed by Brunel and opened in 1854, it originally had three sections of impressive archwork. Here the ends of Brunel's arches can be seen with a fourth on the left being added in 1914. Platforms have had to be extended to accommodate longer trains. In 1998 overhead electrification was added. To clear the bridges, tracks have been lowered by around 600mm.

Opposite below: The current office infill between the great towers of Cannon Street Station makes for an uneasy partnership. The station was in the front line in wartime which led to the downfall of the original roof. The glass suffered partial damage and had to be removed for the sake of safety – but never got replaced. Fifteen years later the frame of the original roof was removed.

CHAPTER 1

CHARING CROSS

When the South Eastern Railway (SER) got its connection to London Bridge, it found that it could expand its ambitions to get right into the heart of London's West End – the capital's theatre district.

With the widening of the brick viaduct approaching London Bridge Station, there was room to branch around that station and take a line westward to meet and connect with Waterloo Station, and then go further to cross the river to Charing Cross. An intermediate station at Waterloo East was included.

There was already a bridge here, one built by Isambard Kingdom Brunel. This was a suspension bridge, but of the type that wouldn't be suitable for a railway. Just beyond the suspension bridge was Hungerford Market.

These railway companies nearly always got what they wanted. The suspension bridge went, as well as the market. The replacement bridge is the present Hungerford Bridge, a girder structure on cast iron piers. The bridge, before it was widened further, provided four tracks into the station which then had six platforms. There are two huge side walls on which an arched glazed roof was supported. The station at the bridge end is at a higher level than the road, because the ground rises away from the Embankment to the higher level at the Strand.

The fine hotel at the front was constructed soon after the station was completed (designed by E.M. Barry), but unlike some of the other station hotels had a decent forecourt. The cross that can be seen today is a reconstruction of a memorial cross to Queen Eleanor by King Edward I in 1290. The original was destroyed by Puritans.

Charing Cross became the most central of all the terminus stations. So central that it is the point where all distances from London are measured. The road which passes in front is the A4, the Strand. Once opened, the station, being so central, became the terminus for continental boat trains linking with the Dover ferries. Even Thomas Cook had a sales office there in the early days.

The station kept its boat trains until the early 1900s when the SER merged with its previous arch rival, the London Chatham & Dover Railway (LC&DR) to become the South Eastern & Chatham Railway (SE&CR). A setup which would remain until the government sponsored the 'Grouping' of all railway companies in 1923 into just four companies. The system slowly became electrified with the Southern Railway (SR) adopting a third rail conductor.

Disaster struck the station in 1905 when part of the roof collapsed. The curved roof was replaced by a glazed ridge-and-furrow type which covered the platforms and concourse. It butted up to the back of the hotel. Much later, when the space above the station was developed, only the concourse retained a glazed roof.

After massive usage in the second half of the 1800s, the platforms were extended onto the bridge. It was not until 1884, when the Circle Line was completed along the Embankment that there was any easy form of movement across London for the general public. Hence the above-ground connection between Charing Cross and Cannon Street was well used. Even the main line trains from Charing Cross looped around to Cannon Street before proceeding on their journey.

By the 1860s the rail system had improved dramatically. Signalling became efficient with the introduction of signal boxes at each rail section, with starter signals to see trains away from the station. The newly amalgamated SE&CR quickly reorganised the redirection of boat train services to come and go from Victoria, among many other things.

The Grouping happened after the railways had come under government control during World War I. At the time of handing back to the former private companies, major changes and restructuring were needed. The station then became part of the SR.

Like all the south-facing stations, Charing Cross became a strategic location through both wars of the twentieth century. It caught bombs in World War II when the hotel was put out of action by firebombs. The bridge took several hits including a rocket impacting the south side in 1944.

The 'Cross' is a tribute to the original cross which was erected on this site by Edward I as one of thirteen such crosses which commemorated the memory of his wife Eleanor after her death in 1290. The original was destroyed in 1647 after which there was a wait until 1864 when this new example was constructed. All measurements of distance from London are taken from this location. Hence the station is the most central of all London terminus stations. In the background is the Charing Cross Hotel designed by E.M. Barry.

Above: The office development above the station stretches back as far as the glazed roof above the station concourse. The site has certainly been exploited due to its status as the most central London terminus. It is modern business practice to squeeze as much square footage of office space into a site as it can stand. The only concession to the original design is the curved roof. The road along the Embankment is above the Circle and District Lines of the Underground.

Opposite above: Hungerford Bridge was always the ugliest and noisiest railway bridge in London. The new walkways on both sides, with the cable supports, largely eliminate the poorness of the original design. This site was originally home to a suspension bridge designed by Brunel. The bases of this can be seen because they were reused for the new bridge.

Opposite below: By comparison, the structure above Cannon Street Station seems quite modest. Here is Terry Farrel's design and construction of the late 1980s. The initials SR give a tribute to the former Southern Railway, which took over from the regional private companies in 1923. In former days the trains were shorter, but now the platforms have to stretch above the river.

To the south side of the river the lines pass close to the Royal Festival Hall. Built for the 1951 Festival of Britain exhibition, the hall had to be incredibly well insulated against the noisy Hungerford Bridge. During the Festival, the 'Skylon', 'Shot Tower' and part of the 'Dome of Discovery' would have been seen in this view. The brick arches take the railway lines onwards and also beyond London Bridge Station to Greenwich. The bridge beyond is Waterloo Bridge.

A 1905 postcard gives a feel of times gone by. The horse buses would rarely have exceeded 6mph, so walking would have been just as quick. A Bureau de Change at the bottom right indicates that the station's central location would have been exploited for continental travel. Thomas Cook, the man who first put together the idea of 'day excursions' had an office on the right-hand side. An ideal starting point for a day out to one of the new resorts on the south coast.

An artist must have touched in the brick faces shown on the postcard. The modern-day photograph shows the construction is of London Stock yellow brickwork. The top two floors were rebuilt in 1951. Unlike some of the stations, this one does have a useful dropping-off forecourt for travellers. Cars and taxis wait at a red signal before rushing on their way. The Strand Underground station was situated on the right within the forecourt, but deemed surplus to requirements and removed.

The front of the concourse is just behind the hotel. The original balcony and first floor reception rooms are above the clock and can be seen in early prints. The depth of the hotel takes up the ticket offices and other service areas. At one time the concourse was much smaller but after the partial collapse of the original train shed in 1905, the chance was taken to re-plan the whole station layout.

Above: An early print shows the first signal cabin sitting on a gantry, put in when the station opened in 1865. Cabins were sited just beyond the ends of the platforms, but were replaced after the first widening of the bridge in 1888. The siting of the signals above the roof eliminated the need for wire runs as these could be operated directly by rods. However, London was prone to severe fogs, which blinded the train drivers to the signals. Fogmen with detonators had to be on hand to keep the trains running.

Opposite above: The spacious concourse sits between the back of the hotel and the platforms. Concourses are always best with natural lighting, as here. The huge office building replaced the second train shed put in after the roof collapse. This roof was refurbished – as new after the construction of the office building.

Opposite below: Brunel built this suspension bridge in 1848 to connect Waterloo with the Hungerford Market in West Strand. It was designed for foot and light traffic only. Brunel obviously wanted something different from the sameness of other bridges on river. It only lasted fourteen years until the SER received permission to extend into Charing Cross. A new sturdier bridge took its place which gave the engineers John Hawkshaw and William Barlow the idea of using the redundant chains and saddles of this bridge to complete the Clifton Suspension Bridge. That was after Brunel's death in 1859.

The original iron and glass arched roof was designed by John Hawkshaw (who also designed the roof at Cannon Street). Unfortunately part of this roof collapsed during work in 1905, causing many fatalities. The rest of the roof was then removed to be replaced by a simpler ridge and furrow design. The hotel rooms faced directly onto the very smoky train shed. All stations liked a cab road to come through the station. Here it rises from Villiers Street to pass through and discharge the horse-drawn vehicles onto the station forecourt. The two lines each side of this were for boat train traffic.

The replacement station roof can be seen here, which lasted until the construction of the office building, commenced in the late 1980s. The SR replaced the earlier SE&CR after the Grouping of the railways in 1923.

The insignia of the SR (which existed from 1923 to 1948) was not lost to the management after the new office development was completed. The crest shows the arms of some of the locations the railway served. Clockwise, they are London, Brighton, Dover and Southampton.

The original Charing Cross station c. 1897, with a Cudworth 2-4-0 tender locomotive and train comprising non-bogied carriage stock. A Stirling 0-4-4 tank waits with a local suburban service on the left.

A view looking outwards from the station. The bridge extends over the Thames to take the trains to London Bridge and beyond. In former times the signal cabins and gantries would have extended right across the lines, just metres from the platform ends. Today the quiet trains just glide across the once noisy Hungerford Bridge to join the brick arched viaduct system beyond.

CHAPTER 2

EUSTON

The London & Birmingham (L&B) Railway was the first railway company to get a long distance connection to London, in 1837, when Euston opened right up to, but not beyond, New Road (now Euston Road), the boundary across which no lines could venture.

To get to their new site the L&B had to cross the Regent Canal and then make a descent of 1 in 77 for nearly a mile. Fine going down, but those little lightweight steam engines would have problems pulling a loaded train the other way. At this stage any such problem would always be overcome. The trains stopped on the high ground at Chalk Farm where they remained while an ever-moving cable driven by a steam powered pump hauled the carriages up the incline.

This was successful enough, so much so that it stayed in place until 1844. By this time, the company had built the Doric Arch, the Grand Hall and two hotels. All of which shows what an enormously successful industry the railways had become. Other expansions had been made for additional lines, outbuildings, parcels offices, etc.

It very soon became apparent that these marvellous structures, the Euston Arch and the Great Hall, were built in the wrong places. The Arch and its outbuildings restricted the flow of vehicles approaching the station and the Hall completely split the station in two. The company could expand eastward, which they did, up to Eversholt Street and west as far as the parcels office, but there was no chance of anything happening in the middle.

The L&B quickly sold out to the London & North Western Railway (LNWR) which could make the necessary connections to serve the North West and Scotland. The problem was now somebody else's.

Even as early as 1898 there were plans to pull the Hall down, but nothing happened until 1961. The classic Arch stood where it could be seen and admired by passing traffic on the Euston Road. However it soon became hidden when the two hotels decided to join up with each other, thus blocking the approach road and obscuring the Arch. At that time it was not properly appreciated as a piece of fine Doric Greek architecture, whose features demand some space in the front of them. They need to be seen. Once space is closed off, the architecture cannot be appreciated. This happened to the nearby St Pancras Church also. The Euston Arch deserved better appreciation and deserved another chance. The Grand Hall, however, was still in the wrong place and had to go.

The two original lodges beside the Arch were pulled down to make more room for traffic. However, two new lodges (pictured) were then built well forward of the originals. The idea was that because the hotels obscured so much, the lodges would identify the station to traffic on the Euston Road. They are still there, having survived when everything else didn't. These two odd looking structures have found a variety of uses from being tourist information offices to little bars (which one is today). A strange thing about them is that on the corner quoin stones are place names that can be reached from this station, but also a good many which can't. The same thing was done at Blackfriars Station, but that south-facing station could at least fancifully claim services to Marseilles and St Petersburg. At Euston the claims are more modest, as among the names are Rochdale and Peterborough.

If one stood between these two lodges and looked towards the station, a full frontal view of the arch would once have been seen. Now all that is on view is Richard Seifert's 1960's offices with four shiny black boxes on top. Although these too are now are destined to go.

Euston was the starting place of the West Coast Main Line. This grew in opposition to Nigel Gresley's East Coast Main Line. As could be expected, with two private companies becoming rivals, the competitive spirit grew. In the 1930s the great 'named trains' left both King's Cross and Euston at the same time to ply their trade to Glasgow, Edinburgh and beyond. Forty years before this, when locos had become larger, signalling had been perfected and the tracks were of the finest steel, 'races' to Scotland began to get great publicity. That had to stop, owing to the demands put upon man and machine. However, by the 1930s all steam records were getting broken on both railways – never to be bettered.

King's Cross may have had the *Flying Scotsman*, the A4s and the *Silver Jubilee*, But Euston countered with the *Coronation Scot*, the huge Princesses and the classic Duchesses.

The most outlandish of all the streamliners came and went from Euston, always trying to keep up with the LNER and their trains on the East Coast route. William Stanier brought out the 'Princess Coronation' Class with its domed front and painted lining, which went right down the train. Once all this casing was removed after the war, there was the most beautiful of all British locomotives – the Duchesses. The streamlined Duchess here at the National Railway Museum at York is No. 6229 4-6-2 (all engines of this wheel arrangement are called Pacifics), *Duchess of Hamilton*. One of just three that have survived the cutter's torch.

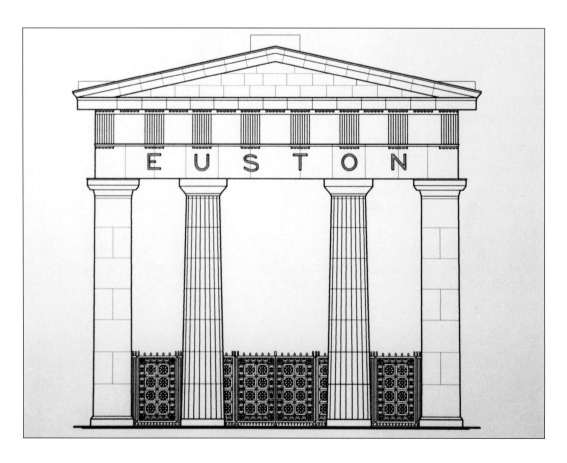

The two pavilions which stand today across the front entrance of Euston Station are not the originals which stood alongside the Doric Arch. These two were erected around 1870 to give more emphasis to the station frontage. The Arch would have been about 100 metres back from here, on the other side of the former Drummond Street. Hotels were built halfway between these pavilions and the Arch, which in the end completely screened the Arch from Euston Road.

The London & North Western Railway Memorial is centred between the two pavilions but placed further back. The great Doric Arch was also on this line, behind where the office development can be seen. The Arch was always a hazard to cabs getting to and from the booking hall, a problem which was never properly solved. All traffic can now get to the front of the station, which is admirably efficient. An approach below the offices leads to the 'new' concourse. The office buildings are on the line of the former hotels. First there was one each side, before a third closed off a view of the Arch.

The Arch will never die, even if some parts of it are at the bottom of a canal in East London. Just along from the bus drop-off point the sign above the pub says it all.

A relic of the Doric Arch does still exist. These are the very gates of the Arch through which the horse-drawn cabs would enter and leave the station, now on show at the National Railway Museum. The space between the gates was found to be inadequate, which led to nearly a century of traffic flow problems.

Euston finally underwent a complete rebuild in the early 1960s. The planning of the 1840s, which had placed the Great Hall right where it shouldn't be, hampered the station for over a century. Unfortunately Euston was redesigned in the worst decade for architecture, the 1960s. But it was a lesson learned. Campaigns to avoid allowing this to happen again saved other stations from the fate of being concreted over.

There is adequate size to the 1962 concourse with full screening to the train area. All very efficient with good communications above the central ticket gates. The only daylight is borrowed from the edges at high level. Corridors come through from below the office building at the front, too far for any borrowed light, although there are sliding doors to avoid wind chill.

Above: With the station needing to be low enough for trains to get under the bridges on the approach and the ticket barriers being at street level, passengers have the less than pleasing experience of taking the slope up and down.

Opposite above: The throat end of the station is out in the open, which is very satisfying, although very few passengers would have any reason to walk this far down the platform. But this experience is fine because there is the chance to see the coming and going of the pride of the West Coast Main Line – the Class 390 'Pendolino'. One or two failed attempts have been made to get a successful tilting train to negotiate the tight bends of Cumbria at high speed. But now the trouble and investment has proved to be worthwhile. The West Coast can still compete.

Opposite below: A view right across the expansion of the station. There is not even a glimpse of how it used to be in the days of steam or before. A complete rebuild removes all history.

Above: Opened in 1846, the Great Hall at Euston represented just where the railways were at. Opulence, style and elegance with absolutely no thought about saving a few pennies here and there. It is an example of a new transport system awash with money, with the owners leaving their mark for centuries to come. The Doric Arch was already built, so this was Part 2 of the grand plan. However, it was not to be. Over the next decade it was shown that these structures were in the wrong place and would impede the expansion of the station. In 1961 it was all pulled down. Note the statue of George Stephenson in the picture.

Opposite above: A print of the first iron train shed which lasted until the 1960 rebuild, although it was subsequently raised by 2 metres. The cables, which pulled the first trains, have gone but the Great Hall can be seen on the left.

Opposite below: A Class 378 dual-voltage train arrives under the Ampthill Square bridge. These government sponsored trains were built by Bombardier for the London overground lines – which consist of a partly new and partly old network which takes in services from north and south. The bridges in front of Euston Station were converted into girder structures around 1900 to make for easier curves into the station. In the early days of cable haulage, just two lines on the extreme right were used – one for arrivals and one for departures. The small carriages could be marshalled within the station on truck-turns.

Above: Various architectural styles appeared in the 1830s in parallel with the development of the railways. The architects and engineers really tried to express themselves, and no more so than here at Euston. They didn't think about great vehicular access or anything like that, just built a monument to show it all off. 'Let's build something which will last four hundred years.' They did, but it only lasted a hundred, because all those cars, taxis and buses had to get in somehow. The architecture of this station was always going to be 'on the run' – and it still is. We now revel in anything historically quirky and unusual and this old arch is up there with the best. At the time a new railway station was thought to be a city in itself, so what it needed was a city gate, just like that of an ancient city.

Left: The George Stephenson statue which was located in the Great Hall, Euston, now resides at the National Railway Museum. Stephenson was one of the four great engineers of the nineteenth century and he advanced the rail industry like no other. Alongside his son Robert, Brunel and George Hudson of the Midland Railway, they were very special industrialists who had the skill and vision to break new ground. In fact it was Robert Stephenson who built the Great Hall and not George, so it is his statue that should have been displayed there.

Opposite: One of the 1870 pair of pavilions which were located forward of the hotels to provide some definition to the entrance. Since then, the hotels have disappeared. Inspiration has been taken from Blackfriars and its set of plaques showing possible destinations (many of them fanciful). Here they tried to be a bit more practical and less glamorous, with destinations such as Rochdale, Swansea, Wigan, Peterborough and Stoke being shown.

Three top link locomotives which used Euston Station from the 1930s.

Above: An engine built in 1930 before all the showmanship of the that decade began. Fast speeds from London to Scotland quickly turned into a competition between the LMS on the West Coast Main Line and the LNER in the East. Streamlining added to all the publicity. No. 46100 *Royal Scot*, seen here at Keighley, had a 7P power rating, meaning that engines had to be changed at Carlisle.

Opposite above: The LNER, with its 'A' Classes, was achieving new record times for the non-stop run from King's Cross to Edinburgh amid great acclaim, so the LMS had to do something about it. William Stanier designed the biggest engine ever to have run in Britain. This is the 'Princess Royal' Class No. 6201 *Princess Elizabeth*, in the crimson lake livery the LMS kept for their top engines. The design did the trick as this very engine, here seen heading a main line special in Suffolk, set a steam record for the 401-mile Glasgow to Euston run in 1936 at an average speed of 70mph.

Opposite below: The finest class of engine ever to grace Euston Station. No other loco looked so good even if it was just standing there. The classic LMS 'Duchess' No. 46233 *Duchess of Sutherland* is one of the Coronation Class built in 1938 when it had the streamlined casing. This was removed after the war to aid operational maintenance. One of three which have been preserved, *Duchess of Sutherland* is on show and shown here working at the Midland Railway Centre, Butterley.

CHAPTER 3

BLACKFRIARS

Many different railway companies fancied getting use of the north–south direct route through London. But it was the LC&DR that achieved this in those early, heady days of railway expansion. The LC&DR saw off their great rival, the SER, which had got to Charing Cross and the nearby Cannon Street, but that station had no through route.

The link at Blackfriars was completed in 1866, but firstly the LC&DR had to build a station on the south side of the river. In 1864 the company constructed a substantial building to establish a service with lines connecting to it from the Elephant and Castle and beyond. At the same time the bridge across the river was under construction (the one with the iron piers.)

Always the aim was to link with the Metropolitan lines at Farringdon, and then go westward and join with King's Cross and St Pancras stations, which had connections for these services. Another curve was made eastward to make the short distance to Moorgate, a terminus that was much closer to the City of London – the financial heart of the Empire.

The Blackfriars railway bridge was completed by the end of 1864 and the LC&DR connected it with a new high-level station just before Ludgate Hill.

The new station took over from the former station on the South Bank, serving both the financial district and the newspaper industries in Fleet Street. Immediately the connection with Farringdon was put under construction, requiring a sharp descent to be made at 1 in 39 to bring the lines down to the lower level.

After opening in 1866, the north–south connections had massive usage, so much so that it became necessary to build the Blackfriars terminus station just to the north side of the river (called St Paul's until 1937). This could then also serve the through passenger services. This in turn required a second bridge which was constructed at the same time.

A further station was soon required. This was built from a spur at high level to become Holborn Viaduct Station, which opened in 1875. It became the terminus for services to the immediate southern areas before it closed in 1990.

Massive use of this north–south connection was made by goods traffic, it being the only crossover line for the capital. It was an essential serving line, especially in wartime, when goods had to be taken to the south coast ports in great quantities.

The bigger picture of how these lines and services evolved is detailed in the book *London's Termini* by Alan A. Jackson (now sadly out of print but available second-hand).

The north–south passenger services across London ground to a halt in the first half of the twentieth century. That smoky climb, within the tunnel between Farringdon and Ludgate Hill, had proven a killer. However, no one wanted this service go away and with the coming of electric trains, the problem was solved.

In 1988, a through passenger train service from Bedford to Brighton was put on the table under the overall banner of 'Thameslink'. It had been a bugbear to the rail planners that passengers wishing to get from the counties north of London to those in the south always came up against the barrier of all the big stations stopping the trains dead at the buffers. An underground ride around the Circle Line was needed to overcome the barrier between Euston Road and the River Thames.

There were to be rationalisations. The underused terminus of Holborn Viaduct was to go, as was the high-level station at Ludgate Hill. From this location a new low-level tunnel could be constructed to Blackfriars station and the original bridge across Ludgate Hill would be redundant. It was demolished in 1991. Much more valuable office space was made available, providing some of the revenue for the project. The notorious 'steam tunnel' north of Ludgate Hill went along with Holborn Viaduct Station, and Ludgate Hill became a low-level facility. The new tunnel up to Blackfriars was steep (1 in 39), but absolutely no problem for the sleek and clean electric trains.

New stations, better signalling, new tracks and trains were all developments that made the operator, Network Rail, thrive. Government funding followed, to take the improvements all the way, with virtually new stations being built at Blackfriars and London Bridge. Both of these stations are now a pleasure to use rather the product of ongoing changes, as they used to be.

Blackfriars is now a wonder in itself, for the new platforms completely spread across the Thames. A view to the east on a sunny day is something to behold, taking in all the river traffic, with Tower Bridge in the background. It all links with the South Bank walk, which must be one of the ten best walks in the country. The iron piers of the former bridge have been repainted, having been filled with lean-mix concrete and topped off with mortar. Four thousand solar panels make up the roof of the new station, providing half of the station's electricity needs.

So successful is the Thameslink service that destinations now showing in the timetables include King's Lynn and Peterborough to the north, and Eastbourne and Ashford in the south.

A poster of the time entitled 'Across River'.

Left: Blackfriars station now takes up the whole of the 1885 bridge and 400 solar panels provide almost 50 per cent of the station's electricity needs. Both this bridge and the original worked side by side for about a century, but for long periods passenger services did not run. This was probably due to steam engines on passenger trains having to climb a 1 in 39 slope within tunnels. Now, with electric trains, passenger services thrive.

Below: The cast iron supports of the original (1865) bridge remain as a tribute to the past. The bridge became redundant when the four necessary through tracks could be accommodated on the 1885 structure. Although this was widened over one set of c.i. piers. Before 1986 the long-standing Blackfriars terminus station would have been visible in the distance on the north side. Now the station crosses the river completely, making it unique to the capital. The first terminus was on the south side and, after a couple of years, connected with the bridge in the foreground.

The year given on the plaque confirms the building of this first bridge. Constructed in cast iron there was one at each end on the west side. This clearly showed the passers by on the adjacent road bridge what this company was all about. Now there is only one plaque visible; the other has been placed behind this, facing inwards to the new station.

The first Blackfriars Station on the north side (which was called St Paul's) was a little on the 'less than glamorous' side. To counteract this, the LC&DR installed a set of pink/red stones with the names of 54 towns and cities which could (only in their minds) be reached from this station. It was one of those things which was so quirky it had to be reassembled within the new station.

Above: A view which cannot be bettered from any other London station. From halfway down the platform, the comings and goings of London's river can be observed. Four bridges stand before Tower Bridge. They are: Millennium Footbridge, Southwark Bridge, Cannon Street Rail Bridge and London Bridge.

Opposite above: Halfway down the station the brightness of the location is apparent. Rooflights between the solar panels give an airy ambience to the new station. Four tracks and four platforms cross the river with passenger access at both ends.

Opposite below: With The Black Friar pub just visible in the distance, the new station frontage takes its place on the corner of the approach road to the Blackfriars road bridge. There is a fine interlink with the Underground District Line here, which also serves the Circle Line. As can be seen from the next picture, the station is at the level above, which leaves the lines upwards or downwards accessible by escalators. The line dives two levels to get underground towards Farringdon.

Above: A great view from the Shard shows the extent of the new Blackfriars Station. It crosses the river on the 1865 bridge and just behind can be seen the Blackfriars road bridge. The millennium footbridge is in the foreground connecting the South Bank with St Paul's Cathedral.

Opposite above: The new bridge going northwards from Blackfriars is already descending as it crosses Queen Victoria Street. Right in the heart of everything is a good old surviving pub: The Black Friar. This is the only main line ever to connect north and south through Central London. Early planning restrictions prevented this, but it has always been a mighty cross-route, especially for goods. Through the wars it kept everything moving, but these days that traffic gets diverted to the east and west avoiding lines.

Opposite below: A Thameslink train disappears downwards to get from station level to sub-road at Ludgate Hill. Previous to the 1986/1991 works the trains would have crossed Ludgate Hill on the bridge, now removed (but a postcard in this book shows it), before descending to Farringdon at a slope of 1 in 39. There was also a spur to the now defunct Holborn Viaduct station. Note that the Southern third rail system has crossed the river and is used here. It goes as far as Farringdon before the train transfers to the overhead power wires.

Above: A view looking south across the Blackfriars road bridge. This *London Weekly News* print shows the first and very short-lived Blackfriars Station on the south side of the river. Note the girder railway bridge adjoining the station, with the piers and plaque which are still there. Back in the 1850s the London port was the largest and busiest in the world, so the level of river traffic shown here is accurate. This impressive station opened in 1864 and ceased being a passenger terminus in 1866 when the railway got the river crossing.

Opposite above: Ludgate Hill railway bridge was always part of the London scene until it suddenly disappeared in 1991. Now the trains go underground, although there is a station here called City Thameslink. The London traffic was always mighty slow and congested in days gone by. Traffic lights didn't properly come into use until 1926. Before that, policemen on point duty did their best to control things.

Opposite below: Blackfriars Terminus Station, then called St Paul's (until 1937), with an ex-SE&CR F1 4-4-0 tender locomotive and train at the platform, c. 1935.

A look back at Blackfriars Station at the time of an enthusiasts' farewell rail tour. The through lines are on the left. The Thameslink developments of the late 1980s led to the removal of the terminus facility.

CHAPTER 4

LONDON BRIDGE

In 1840, four private railway companies had established the use of London Bridge Station. The first was the L&GR which paved the way and thus controlled everything. Even the London, Brighton and South Coast Railway (LB&SCR) took the opportunity to get in there. They wanted to get their connection to the City of London. Each of the companies had two tracks and they built separating walls to further establish their territory.

All being steam powered by very primitive locomotives and on wrought iron rails, the L&GR became the first company to open a London terminus right into the centre of the city. It was just six years since the enthusiasm had begun to build concerning railways, leading to lines popping up all over the land. With amalgamations and companies doing their own thing it had taken less than a decade for a network to be established. The government encouraged it all by offering little resistance, for it was the building of these railways which was bringing the country out of a devastating economic slump and into a new age of prosperity. People from the country began to come to the towns in large numbers.

The arch viaduct from Greenwich gave the landowners continued access below the railway. These arches also provided enclosed lettable spaces for stabling and warehouses, etc., much later being enthusiastically used by the motor trade.

The new terminus at London Bridge was a Spartan affair, being the butt end of the viaduct with an adjoining office building. The platforms were open to the elements, but that could be sorted out later, and all the publicity was in favour of the pioneering L&GR.

The second company that wanted to join the L&GR with routes into the city was the London & Croydon Railway (L&CR) (getting into the capital allowed it to add the prestigious 'London' to its title). This company needed to swing round from its southerly base and join the viaduct from New Cross. The L&GR then charged this new user by taking a cut of their ticket sales and promptly added another twin track viaduct next to their own to accommodate this. Later, when the SER also wanted to come in, another twin track viaduct was built on the north side.

In 1839 the L&CR and the L&GR constructed a new and elaborate joint station. The SER had negotiated terms to use the north side of the enlarged site, building a separating wall between them and their entrenched rivals. The SER was horrified at the costs being charged by Greenwich, so much so that it took a spur off the Croydon line to set up a terminus at the Bricklayers Arms site to offer a commercial challenge. This stayed in existence until 1845 when the SER became firmly established at London Bridge and finally absorbed the L&GR. Bricklayers Arms then became solely a long-standing goods facility.

The Croydon and Brighton companies also merged a year later to become the LB&SCR, taking over the south side terminus station. The SER then had eyes on stretching further into central London to Charing Cross and Cannon Street in the mid-1860s. This involved building a difficult extended line westward, firstly breaking through Borough Market and then going on to pass Waterloo Station and make the river crossing to Charing Cross. Also built at this time was the triangle of lines at Borough, with the river crossing link to Cannon Street.

The constant changes at London Bridge left the whole site with a haphazard layout which caused operating difficulties right through to the second half of the twentieth century.

View from the Shard showing the east side of London Bridge Station, with the elevated trackwork heading in from Kent and the coastal resorts. The London & Greenwich Railway was the first company to get into the capital in 1836 with a 876-arch viaduct providing just two tracks. Very soon three other companies had negotiated access, requiring two more width expansions. The final through route towards Charing Cross came in 1901, bringing the total number of lines to eleven.

London Bridge Station benefited greatly from the government sponsored Thameslink 2010–2015 investment, when the whole station was refurbished. The remodelling brought a ramshackle station into the twenty-first century. Here at platform level, all the canopies have been replaced, with escalator connections to the central concourse. A Hastings-bound train glides off eastwards along the viaduct, taking a service from Charing Cross.

Coming off the Thameslink river crossing from Blackfriars, the train on the right has arrived from St Albans to the north of London. It has taken the underground branch before St Pancras to meet the lines of the Metropolitan, before branching off at Farringdon to cross the river and arrive at London Bridge. The bi-voltage train would have discarded its connections to the overhead wires at Farringdon and switched to the Southern third rail system.

From 1859 the SER gained approval to extend past London Bridge and add a new terminus at Charing Cross. This meant extending the viaduct northwards again. The modern view of the bypassing platforms shows it finally ended up with nine tracks. The last widening was carried out in 1901.

Opposite above: The departure board now shows trains from Bedford to the north going to the south coast resorts of Hastings and Brighton. The nine through platforms on the north side allow for trains not only from Charing Cross but also from Waterloo East, Cannon Street, Blackfriars, Farringdon, King's Cross and St Pancras. The revived Thameslink passenger connections have done wonders for the station as part of the modernisation plan.

Opposite below: The brick arches fronting onto Tooley Street are from the final northward extension of the station in 1901. These arches joined the others to make up the ongoing eleven-track viaduct towards Greenwich. The early arches were useful as stables, workshops or for storage. Modern-day uses include gift shops and cafés.

Departures

Special Notices

11:15og

CUSTOMER INFORMATION

CUSTOMERS REQUIRING
PLATFORMS 1 TO 9

PLEASE GO STRAIGHT
DOWN THE ESCALATORS
ON THE LEFT AND
TURN LEFT AT THE
BOTTOM.

Departures

11:19	Bedford	
	Expt 11:25	Plat 5
11:19	via Gatwick Airport	
	On time	Plat 11
11:19	via Tulse Hill	
	On time	Plat 15
11:24	& Tattenham Corner	
	On time	Plat 13
11:35	via Tulse Hill	
	On time	Plat -
11:38	Crystal Palace	
	On time	Plat 14
11:41	Three Bridges	
	On time	Plat 4
11:49	via Tulse Hill	
	On time	Plat -

Page 1 of 2

Departures

11:49	Bedford	
	Expt 11:50	Plat 5
11:54	& Tattenham Corner	
	On time	Plat -
12:05	via Tulse Hill	
	On time	Plat -
12:08	Crystal Palace	
	On time	Plat -
12:11	Three Bridges	
	On time	Plat 4
12:19	via Gatwick Airport	
	On time	Plat -
12:19	via Tulse Hill	
	On time	Plat -
12:19	Bedford	
	On time	Plat 5

Page 2 of 2

Departures

11:17	Charing Cross	
	Due	Plat 9
11:19	Hastings	
	On time	Plat 7
11:19	Bedford	
	Expt 11:25	Plat 5
11:19	Horsham	
	On time	Plat 11
11:19	East Croydon	
	On time	Plat 15
11:21	Dartford	
	On time	Plat 6
11:21	Charing Cross	
	Due	Plat 8
11:24	Charing Cross	
	Due	Plat 9

Page 1 of 2   **11:15:08**

Above: Platform 10 is the first of six serving the terminus side of the station. It has all the smooth passenger flow facilities which are integral to today's station. All signs of the old, hotchpotch arrangements have disappeared. The early history of the station, with four or five companies vying for the best positions, created a century and a half of awkwardness in its wake. No trace is left of that situation other than its legacy we can now appreciate.

Opposite: The Shard is the tallest building in Europe. Constructed at the same time as the London Bridge Station renovations, the two sit well together. From the three viewing floors, many London stations can be appreciated as well as the views right across the capital's flatlands. The airiness around the open platforms at London Bridge makes this station one of the most pleasant to use. Architectural planning has come a long way.

Above: Unlike Waterloo where the concourse is on a higher level, here it has to be at street level. The new enlarged area connects all parts of the station including access to the Northern Line. Excellent signage and information boards provide passengers with all the information they need.

Opposite above: This train is proceeding over the Cannon Street triangle from Charing Cross. This particular line is the 1901 addition, when the new set of elevated tracks crashed through Borough Market. All Cannon Street trains now take the sweep into and through London Bridge. In former days the connection from Cannon Street to Charing Cross was well used. Before the Underground lines arrived on the north side of the river, this was the quickest way for the public to get from the City of London to the West End.

Opposite below: London Bridge terminus as it was before the complete rebuilding changed everything. The through lines sit to the right of the separating wall. Many companies shared this space in the early days, beginning with the L&GR in 1836 – the first main line to come into Central London.

Opposite above: An early view from the east looking towards the station. Gantries like these were used at Charing Cross, Waterloo and Cannon Street Stations before persistent London fogs brought signalling nearer ground level. Note the two-way signals on each post.

Opposite below: The outside of London Bridge c. 1895 looking towards the main entrance. The vehicles have come up the ramp from road level to access the buildings of three railway companies. The L&GR was the first to arrive here in 1836, to be closely followed by the LB&SCR and then the SER. Some grudging sharing took place but inside there were separating walls keeping most operations apart. Lines also passed by on the north side, so not surprisingly the station was never a favourite for its ease of use.

The front entrance to London Bridge is at viaduct level. One of the columns of the Shard building goes right through the forecourt. The bus pick-up and set-down facility is also at this level. The architectural aspect can be appreciated where the alternative may have been to obliterate the station with a low-rise block covering the whole area.

From the Cannon Street triangle the lines head on westward towards Waterloo and Charing Cross. A line can be seen crossing over here. This goes from Blackfriars towards Elephant and Castle and beyond. There is also an easterly connection from the Blackfriars line used for the north/south Thameslink services.

CHAPTER 5

CANNON STREET

The SER had finally achieved a through route past London Bridge Station and in 1863 took it westward across the river into Charing Cross. A magnificent achievement.

The SER then saw its rivals, the LC&DR, gain permission to cross the river to Blackfriars, which it achieved in 1866. That is where the SER also wanted to be – across the river, closer to the financial district which is the City of London. The planning had already been done with the building of the triangle of lines at Borough. All this was on the brick viaduct which linked nicely with the new railway bridge across the Thames.

The SER was actually the first to get across the river, beating the LC&DR by months in 1866. The only other station to be built in the City of London was Fenchurch Street, which opened in 1841. Remember, this was still during those mad early days of railway euphoria.

The new bridge to Cannon Street provided five tracks across the river, with the bridge supported on four sets of four sturdy stone pillars. The station was right on the edge of the river, having nine tracks entering it. The outer tracks were singles with an internal facing platform, and then there were three sets of double track entries. There was one additional shorter line that would have been a siding for the engines. Beyond the shorter entry, a cab road ran part way into the station.

The station opened four years before the District Line was completed. This was part of what was to become the Circle Line which ran below street level and eventually connected nearly all the London terminus stations. It was finished in 1884.

With the SER owning this station and also Charing Cross it was able to make a connection to provide a seven-minute ride between the two stations. The only other option for the general public was to board a horse bus which, with stops, wouldn't travel at much more than walking pace. So successful did this little circular ride prove, crossing the river twice, that it stayed in existence until 1926 when third-rail electrification came in. Even all the boat trains came into Cannon Street from Charing Cross before going on their way. A second bigger engine would then take the train onwards after it had backed in. The platforms to the station were remodelled and extended to take the longer trains.

After electrification, Victoria Station picked up all the boat train services which left Cannon Street largely as a station for commuters. Steam engines generally provided some longer distance services. After 1923, all southern services had been grouped to become the SR. Steam and the electric ran side by side until the end of steam for this station in 1962.

A stylish five-storey hotel had been built at the street end, designed by E.M. Barry to be a station hotel with offices on the ground floor. This operated until 1931 when it couldn't survive the economic slump and was forced to close. Widening the bridge occurred along the way, with five more lines being added and two more support piers built to supplement the existing sets of four.

Wartime didn't treat the station well, with bombs hitting the hotel building and part of the glazed roof. So hazardous was the falling glass that it was decided to remove the remainder until better times and store it in a warehouse. Unfortunately the stored glass did not survive the war and the remaining iron structure of the roof was left unattended for more than a dozen years. Eventually there was no option other than to remove the whole structure. In the late 1950s and early 60s just the two bookend-type walls stood there, as if a monument to war.

The sensible view then was to take a commercial approach and sell the space above the station for office development. The result is what you see today, an unhappy merging of the new with the old.

The station lost its iron and glass roof to the war effort. The glass was removed and stored but never got replaced. With the arch and screen lattice being left unattended for nearly twenty years, rot set in. There was no other option than to remove the whole structure. By this time, the rents achievable for office space in the City reflected the decisions made.

Cannon Street Station as seen from the Shard. The tight site requires the platforms to project onto the bridge over the Thames. A roof garden is clearly visible on what is quite a modest office development over the station. There is a taller block behind, fronting onto the street. Little thought was given to providing any natural light within the station although the concourse does borrow some daylight from the street.

The view from the South Bank shows the station to be right on the river. The office buildings in the background include the Cheese Grater, the Walkie Talkie and the Gherkin. They all sit in the famous Square Mile which is the City of London, the long-time centre of world finance. The two brick towers of the station have survived all bombing raids as have the massive brick side walls.

Further along from the last picture, the influence of Christopher Wren's masterpiece St Paul's Cathedral can be appreciated rather than that of the modern skyline. The railway bridge now has six sets of massive stone piers where there were just four before the bridge was widened at the turn of the 1900s. Electrification was added in 1922 when steam and electric trains ran side by side until 1962.

Southwark Bridge and Cannon Street rail bridge are in the foreground, with the Millennium footbridge further on, linking the South Bank with St Paul's Cathedral. The Tate Modern Gallery is just to the left. This view takes in two stations, with Blackfriars railway bridge being the furthest away. Blackfriars links with lines going onwards belowground to become the Thameslink service.

Around the western side, the Underground station gets its own entrance. With stunning architecture overhead, even the District and Circle lines have benefited from the recent upgrading.

Above: Looking outwards from the concourse, there is plenty of circulation space both coming in from the street and the Underground station.

Opposite: The stairs into the concourse of the main station only require a few steps, thereby allowing the concourse to borrow a good amount of natural light. The concourse is at the same level as the railway bridge.

SR Schools Class locomotive No. 925 *Cheltenham*, which was a typical mid-range engine running from this station. The class was designed by the SR chief mechanical engineer, Richard Maunsell and entered traffic in 1935. They had a narrow width to allow them to pass through the extremely narrow tunnels on the Hastings line. Three out of the original forty have survived into preservation.

Above: Cannon Street around 1906 with a Wainwright 4-4-0 tender locomotive about to depart the station for the Kent coast. Note the extended timber platform.

Opposite above: A post-war view of Cannon Street where the glass has been absent from the roof for over fifteen years – hence all the ironwork has rotted. Ready to depart is King Arthur Class LSWR/SR N15 locomotive No. 30806 *Sir Galleron* with a service to the Kent coast. The date of this picture is 5 June 1958. An electric suburban stock train departs the other platform.

Opposite below: Cannon Street Station hotel suffered bomb damage in World War II with the station roof receiving partial damage. Hence, all the glazing was removed for safety reasons, but was never replaced afterwards. Here, on 11 June 1959, the rebuilt West Country Class Pacific 34001 *Exeter* sits alongside a narrow-bodied Hastings diesel/electric unit. The remains of the roof have recently been removed. The space left by the roof's removal looks very inviting for some high-end lettable office space!

CHAPTER 6

WATERLOO

Between the wars, Waterloo Station's esteem was not good. There is one particular reason for which this discomfort was being felt: Waterloo Bridge. The problem was that the old bridge across the Thames began to subside, enough for cracks to appear in the superstructure. So much so, that in the 1920s the bridge actually closed. A single carriageway steel bridge was erected to the north side but this could only take traffic going one way – southbound. This appalling situation carried on all through the 1930s, leaving the passengers who wanted to get directly to the north side of the river with some poor options. Any bus or taxi connection would have to use the adjacent Westminster or Blackfriars bridges. Foot traffic could have used the skimpy walkway to the side of Hungerford Bridge. There were the two underground lines, the Northern and City services, but for people with luggage this was not a good option.

The only solution was to knock the old bridge down and start again with something good and wide. This thankfully was done and, in wartime, done well. It became the Waterloo Bridge that we see and use today. A top architect, Sir Giles Gilbert Scott, was commissioned to design the structure which survives as the most modern looking road bridge in town.

All the previous north–south bus services, and more, could be reinstated. Waterloo could finally be itself, the biggest and best station in the country. Certainly the only major main line station to the south of the river.

Waterloo serves the South West of the country and rather than compete with the other southern companies, its great competitor was the GWR. In those turn of the century days, the great thing was communications with America. The longstanding company which operated from Waterloo was the London & South Western Railway (L&SWR). Along with the GWR, it wanted the lucrative passenger and mail trade which dropped off at Plymouth. This rivalry even developed into 'races', in the same way that the 'races to the North' that began in the 1890s. However, at the outbreak of war in 1914 the government took control of all the railways. After the war, the entire network was in such a run-down state that the whole country was grouped into just four railway companies. In 1923 everything to the south became the SR, until 1948 when it became the Southern Region following nationalisation.

In the early days, all these South London railways favoured building above road level on a series of brick arches. This eliminated the problem of road crossings, always a bane of railway construction. Overbridges solved that problem very nicely. As previously noted, the arches acted as useful storage spaces or, as governments soon realised, an ideal location for small businesses. All of which was good for an expanding economy.

Like all the big terminus stations, there would have been an initial terminus built first, a little way out. Sure enough, as early as 1838 the pioneering Southampton Railway got to put 'London' in front of its name by getting to Nine Elms and constructing a stylish station. It was a good location that linked up with the river. Those early passengers could get a river trip to the City rather than rely on horse-drawn buses travelling on ash-covered roads.

It is always useful to build up services while taking time to review future options, for by 1845 the L&SWR had taken over. It had eyes on going further than Waterloo, perhaps to Cannon Street. Meanwhile, a double set of brick arches had been approved to get to where they were now. The SER provided a connection to its Charing Cross line going eastward and in 1876 built the station which is was has always been known as Waterloo East.

The connection with the SER didn't work, and Waterloo reverted to being a terminus. The connection also closed, leaving just a passenger crossover which is still there today.

Waterloo officially opened in 1848 and at the end of the century got its connection to the City in the form of an Underground line which was soon nicknamed 'The Drain' (the Waterloo & City line).

Nine Elms continued to be used for certain passenger needs, but was also ideal for carriage storage and later became a locomotive workshop and turn-round point. This area was heavily damaged in World War II, and this, along with the demise of the steam engine, meant it never fully recovered to justify its existence. In the 1960s it was taken over and became the site of the relocated Covent Garden fruit and flower market.

The brick-arched viaduct was widened in stages with the final arrangement being completed after major refurbishments at the start of the twentieth century. Electrification came to the station with the SR's plan to go all electric in stages, although this was slow. The third rail reached Brighton in 1933 but Bournemouth was not reached with electric power until 1957. This does show how important the steam engines continued to be. It was from Waterloo that the last steam train ran in 1968. Through all this time there was always the sight of steam and electric working in harness on the Southern.

As a result of all this, powerful steam engines had to be continually developed. Maunsell took over the designs in the 1920s with his famous 'Maunsell Moguls' (2-6-0 wheel arrangement). But it was the eccentric Oliver Bulleid, who took over in 1937, who caused the most interest. He designed three classes of 'Pacific' (4-6-2 wheel arrangement) which were like nothing ever seen before. They had air-smoothed casings which were an attempt to get in on the streamlining fad of the 1930s. The largest of these engines were the Merchant Navy Class, designed to haul the heavy boat trains to the Southampton Ocean Terminal. The most renowned of the electric trains was the *Bournemouth Belle*. This comprised a classic Pullman set of coaches which brought top-class style to the railway.

The station roof at Waterloo is of the ridge and furrow arrangement and was fitted in the first two decades of the twentieth century, covering all twenty-one platforms. The roof is unlike those of the other major stations of the capital, in that it is not constructed in the form of iron archwork. The glazed ribs are aligned crossways to the line of the platforms. This is a very successful design and provides better natural light than at any of the other stations.

The final development was when Waterloo was chosen to be the initial London terminus for the international Eurostar trains. The former Windsor lines (18–21) were taken over for this, with a dramatic new structure being designed over those lines by Nicholas Grimshaw & Partners. This was in use until 2007 when St Pancras took over these services. The one drawback Waterloo had in its operation of these high-speed

trains was that the services had no suitable trackwork to take the trains into Kent. They had to trundle along the old brick-arched structure before connecting with the Eurostar lines near Dartford. The lines below the Grimshaw structure have now reverted back for service as the Windsor lines.

A view from the passageway linking Waterloo East with the main station – just about the only place a picture can be taken of the station's main frontage. Trains from Charing Cross rumble by with the four tracks expanding to seven for the river crossing. A better view of the station can be had from one of these trains, although there is nowhere that the whole station frontage can be seen, which is of course above brick arch level.

Opposite: The opening for the former taxi-way can be seen past the clock. Waterloo is the busiest station in the country with people always seemingly in a hurry. Under the clock has traditionally been the meeting point; one of the things that will never change. The concourse is the country's largest which is remarkable with the realisation that all of the station is at an elevated level – built, like most of the South London stations, over brick arches. It first opened in 1848.

The Victory Arch is Waterloo's main entrance. Opened in 1922 together with a major station expansion at that time, the Arch commemorates victory in World War I, 1914–1918. The station played a major part through both major conflicts of the twentieth century, especially with its links to Southampton docks. In the build up to D-Day in June 1944 massive troop movements were necessary for which Waterloo was the key starting point for military personnel.

Like all the stations built in the nineteenth century, all the platforms have had to be extended to accommodate longer trains. Third rail electrification was added from the 1920s and, for the next forty years, steam and electric motive power worked side by side without any hint of trouble. Once steam and all its support systems went, everything settled into a system of smooth and quiet operation. In the foreground is the curved roof formerly occupied by Eurostar.

Above and opposite above: Two posters by Helen McKie, who was commissioned in 1948 to produce these to celebrate the station's centenary. The top picture represents the station in peacetime while the next version, in jigsaw puzzle form, is the station in wartime. The pictures show great attention to detail with an amazing array of characters. Note the openness of the station with the wartime roof being blacked out. The access road for goods and postal vehicles was a necessity. The Merchant Navy Class (built from 1942) received their names in 1945. These represented all the merchant shipping lines that used Southampton docks through wartime. In wartime the engines would have been painted matt black. Waterloo was the preferred station for boat trains going to the Southampton Ocean Terminal. The named trains such as 'The Cunarder' and the West Country 'Atlantic Coast Express' attracted the best locomotives.

Opposite below: The wide vistas of the station have now disappeared, to its detriment. The fully glazed roof ensured that this was the brightest of all the London terminus stations, but that pleasure has been thwarted by the installation of advertising screening along the station's length above the ticket barriers. The goods access road has given way to more station space.

Above: The forecourt of the station has had many alterations throughout the different eras of Waterloo's life. But the four-faced clock has forever been the one meeting place that cannot fail to be recognised. The balcony on the right was added by Network Rail in 2012 and new shopping facilities have been added. A view across the station didn't warrant a consideration.

Opposite above: Just inside the Victory Arch are four bronze 'Roll of Honour' boards to commemorate the names of the L&SWR's employees who gave their lives in World War I. In that war the railwaymen received automatic call-up, whereas in World War II railway jobs were deemed essential and therefore no general call-up to the employees was enforced. In both conflicts it was the women who took up the vital roles to keep the trains moving; 585 lives are honoured here.

Opposite below: Once through the barriers the openness of the station becomes apparent. The screen on the far side designates where the former Eurostar extension started. Attempts have been made to reuse the space inside the Nicholas Grimshaw structure, including it becoming a theatre. A production of Edith Nesbit's *The Railway Children* had a season here in June 2011, when a thousand viewers were seated on each side of a pair of the tracks. The 1870 loco Stirling Single No. 1 was the mechanical star of the show (aided by two diesel shunters).

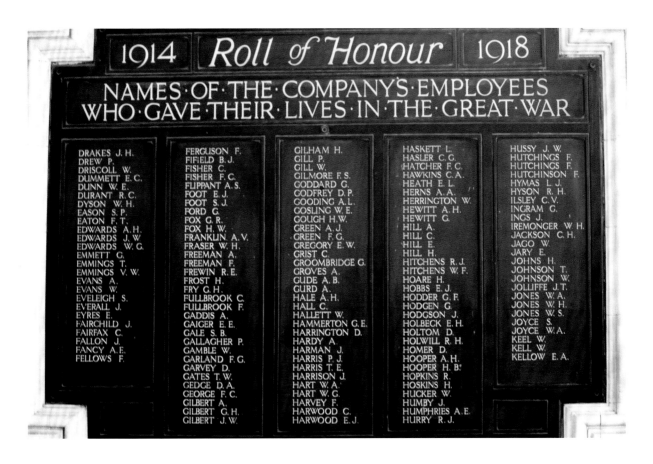

1914 *Roll of Honour* 1918

NAMES·OF·THE·COMPANY'S·EMPLOYEES
WHO·GAVE·THEIR·LIVES·IN·THE·GREAT·WAR

DRAKES J. H.	FERGUSON F.	GILHAM H.	HASKETT L.	HUSSY J. W.
DREW P.	FIFIELD B. J.	GILL P.	HASLER C. G.	HUTCHINGS F.
DRISCOLL W.	FISHER C.	GILL W.	HATCHER F. C.	HUTCHINGS F.
DUMMETT E. C.	FISHER F. C.	GILMORE F. S.	HAWKINS C. A.	HUTCHINSON F.
DUNN W. E.	FLIPPANT A. S.	GODDARD G.	HEATH E. L.	HYMAS L. J.
DURANT R. C.	FOOT E. J.	GODFREY D. P.	HERNS A. A.	HYSON R. H.
DYSON W. H.	FOOT S. J.	GOODING A. L.	HERRINGTON W.	ILSLEY C. V.
EASON S. P.	FORD G.	GOSLING W. E.	HEWITT A. H.	INGRAM G.
EATON F. T.	FOX G. R.	GOUGH H. W.	HEWITT G.	INGS J.
EDWARDS A. H.	FOX H. W.	GREEN A. J.	HILL A.	IREMONGER W. H.
EDWARDS J. W.	FRANKLIN A. V.	GREEN F. G.	HILL C.	JACKSON C. H.
EDWARDS W. G.	FRASER W. H.	GREGORY E. W.	HILL E.	JAGO W.
EMMETT G.	FREEMAN A.	GRIST C.	HILL H.	JARY E.
EMMINGS T.	FREEMAN F.	GROOMBRIDGE G.	HITCHENS R. J.	JOHNS H.
EMMINGS V. W.	FREWIN R. E.	GROVES A.	HITCHENS W. F.	JOHNSON T.
EVANS A.	FROST H.	GUDE A. B.	HOARE H.	JOHNSON W.
EVANS W.	FRY G. H.	GURD A.	HOBBS E. J.	JOLLIFFE J. T.
EVELEIGH S.	FULLBROOK C.	HALE A. H.	HODDER G. F.	JONES W. A.
EVERALL J.	FULLBROOK F.	HALL C.	HODGEN G.	JONES W. H.
EYRES E.	GADDIS A.	HALLETT W.	HODGSON J.	JONES W. S.
FAIRCHILD J.	GAIGER E. E.	HAMMERTON G. E.	HOLBECK E. H.	JOYCE S.
FAIRFAX C.	GALE S. B.	HARRINGTON D.	HOLTOM D.	JOYCE W. A.
FALLON J.	GALLAGHER P.	HARDY A.	HOLWILL R. H.	KEEL W.
FANCY A. E.	GAMBLE W.	HARMAN J.	HOMER D.	KELL W.
FELLOWS F.	GARLAND F. G.	HARRIS P. J.	HOOPER A. H.	KELLOW E. A.
	GARVEY D.	HARRIS T. E.	HOOPER H. B.	
	GATES T. W.	HARRISON J.	HOPKINS R.	
	GEDGE D. A.	HART W. A.	HOSKINS H.	
	GEORGE F. C.	HART W. G.	HUCKER W.	
	GILBERT A.	HARVEY F.	HUMBY J.	
	GILBERT G. H.	HARWOOD C.	HUMPHRIES A. E.	
	GILBERT J. W.	HARWOOD E. J.	HURRY R. J.	

Above: With Waterloo Station at the bottom right of the picture, the footbridge connection to Waterloo East can be seen. The tracks in the picture are coming from London Bridge Station to pass through and cross the river into Charing Cross. In the early days there was a rail connection into the main line station, but with this being at taxi-ramp and concourse level, operating difficulties led to its removal.

Opposite above: A Eurostar train is about to depart Waterloo in 2006, a year before the London starting point was moved to St Pancras International. The service from Waterloo was always hampered by not having a suitable connection to the newly laid lines across Kent. The trains had to trundle around the old style lines passing through places like Beckenham and Bromley before moving to high speed after connection to the express lines near Dartford.

Opposite below: Waterloo Station's main elevation is similar to that at Victoria Station where two buildings make up the frontage. We have a partially brick and stone building built between 1902 and 1906 and the all-stone main entrance finished in 1922. The buildings are perched up at railway bridge level. With the Charing Cross lines passing in front there is no way this architecture can be appreciated or judged from standing back and taking a wider view. The overall road canopy covers the dropping-off point close to the booking hall.

Above: A view of Waterloo Road which via a traffic roundabout leads onto Waterloo Bridge. This has always been the general bus dropping-off and picking-up point for the station with simple stair (and escalator) access onto the concourse. The furthest bridge is the through bridge from Charing Cross. Waterloo East Station is hidden on the right from where the high level footbridge passes over the elevated taxi road to connect with the main concourse at balcony level. The third bridge is the now defunct former rail and footbridge connection from Waterloo East which crossed the taxi road.

Opposite above: Further along Waterloo Road it is clear to see some of the planning problems which faced designers with the station being at high level. The main 'show' frontage is up there, set back to allow for the taxi road to rise and run round. The frontage onto Waterloo Road has left a lot to be desired. A taxi road did at one time run under the covered way before being taken over for passenger circulation.

Opposite below: Taxis and buses use the approach road which rises from York Road – the road linking Waterloo Bridge and Westminster Bridge. There is also the easy river crossing by foot over Hungerford Bridge. This is the best view of the 1922 building with the station's pride and joy, the Victory Arch, nicely in the foreground. The planting which obscures the steps seems to reflect the apathy which surrounds the station's external vistas, although it is a station which is really great. Since the war the public have loved the place for its connections with public transport and the great circulating space inside. Apart from the Victory Arch, it has never really come to terms with its poor appearance from street level.

SR Merchant Navy Class No. 35028 arrives at Clapham Junction to mix with the electric trains, something that always happened for decades back in those steam days. The train on the right has come off the Richmond branch and is heading for Waterloo. All the Merchant Navy locos originally had air-smoothed casings before they were removed in the 1950s.

With the typical styling of Southern locomotives, this example is one of the Lord Nelson Class. Being the prototype, it carries the name *Lord Nelson* and the number 850. The powerful four-cylinder class arrived in the 1920s chiefly to haul the heavy boat trains to and from the Southampton Ocean Terminal. This is the only one which was preserved and is part of the fleet of the Watercress Line in Hampshire.

A class of electric multiple unit which just got on with its work for four decades only to be withdrawn without fanfare. Mundane they might have been, but they performed suburban duties from all of the South London terminus stations. Amazingly, one unit survived into preservation and now looks good at the National Railway Museum. Southern electric 4-sub, original number S58143S, built in 1925.

A scene at Waterloo station c. 1922 with a large number of trains awaiting departure. Third rail electrification had not yet extended to all platforms, although it had been introduced from 1915 – largely covering suburban services.

Above: On 14 August 1956, a rebuilt Merchant Navy Class locomotive waits to take out 'her' service to Plymouth. Originally built with air-smoothed casing in 1945, this engine, like all of the class, had it removed a decade later. The engine is 4-6-2 No. 35013 *Blue Funnel*. Also waiting to depart is the 4 COR electric train unit whose code clearly shows that the destination is Portsmouth.

Opposite above: A Drummond 4-6-0 tender locomotive heads a train of bogie corridor stock at Waterloo c. 1912. This is during the reconstruction of the station which was not completed until 1922.

Opposite below: In one of the outlets at the station, a plaque shows the dedication of a group of women who were determined to give all the support they could to the men fighting for their country.

BETWEEN DECEMBER 1915 AND APRIL 1920 IN THE ARCHES BELOW HERE VOLUNTARY WOMEN WORKERS DISPENSED OVER EIGHT MILLION FREE HOT MEALS AND COMFORTS TO FORCES EITHER GOING TO OR RETURNING FROM THE FRONT. THE HUGE NUMBERS RETURNING WITH THEIR EQUIPMENT MAY NOT HAVE HAD A MEAL OR HOT DRINK FOR UP TO TWELVE HOURS. STATION STAFF HAD ALSO REGULARY WORKED FOR UP TO EIGHTEEN HOURS AT A STRETCH. THE STATION ALSO DEALT WITH AMBULANCE TRAINS AND THOSE PERSONNEL WITH INJURIES.

CHAPTER 7

VICTORIA

On a visit to Victoria Station it soon becomes very obvious that the structure is made up of two buildings. This originates from when this site was first occupied in the period 1860–1862. It was the first time that the railways from the southern counties had crossed the river to have a station close to central London. The LB&SCR was already established at London Bridge but wanted to get its passengers much closer to the West End.

The company completed the right-hand building, as seen from the forecourt, in 1860, building the adjoining Grosvenor Hotel at the same time. This was immediately followed by the LC&DR constructing its building to the left-hand side of the forecourt. Even the GWR got in on the act by bringing in a broad-gauge line which served Windsor, Slough, etc. So we have a Chatham side and a Brighton side, with a sturdy brick wall down the middle of the train area to separate them.

Other south-eastern companies came in, but they had to pay heavy tolls to do so. Even the Grosvenor Railway Bridge had to be widened. Prior to this, both companies had established terminus stations south of the river at Battersea. All the stations south of the river had wanted to use each other's facilities at one time or another, so the conglomeration of lines which had to be built to accommodate this looked like knitting patterns on the south side.

It was a typical situation whereby what was built first quickly became obsolete. Plans were put in place to rebuild both buildings as well as the hotel. The Chatham side was the first to receive the builders with reconstruction being good for occupation in 1906. The Brighton side soon followed with its building being finished in 1908. The new Grosvenor Hotel was also was part of the contract of works. The elevations show that the SE&CR (as it was then) had fancied a stone-clad building of opulent style, which was popular at the time, with Brighton going for a more traditional brick building with stone embellishments. This all took place in the Edwardian period, thought of as the 'Golden Age' of railways. For by this time, the railways had overcome all of the difficulties associated with the progress of a new industry and offered the paying customer comfort and elegance.

Victoria Station had now become the premier place from which to start services to the south coast ports, offering connecting cross-Channel ferry services, i.e. from Dover, Folkestone Newhaven and Southampton. The space and facilities were so much better than at Charing Cross. Waterloo would still serve Portsmouth, Southampton and Plymouth.

During World War I, all the railways were under the control of the government. All luxury and non-essential services were suspended, including Pullman trains. The station, with its continental connections, became the premier departing point for troops being shipped to France from Southampton.

As with all the railways, the war left the infrastructure shattered and run down. Only essential maintenance was done at the stations, and trackwork and rolling stock were left requiring major attention. The numerous private companies couldn't cope, so, as noted earlier, a government-led initiative rationalised everything to create just four companies nationwide. Over 120 small companies had no problem accepting offers of buy-out – compensation for what was by then a set of major problems. Like all the stations dealing with the south of England, Victoria became part of the SR.

With the station now under single ownership, the big separating wall was opened up and arches installed. The signage needed to be changed along with posters and advertising. Some of those old Victorian pieces of cast iron infill showing initials of past owners could stay; nobody would be worried about that.

As with all the SR future plans, electrification using the 600v DC third rail power source was to be phased in, although the steam engines and their supporting needs would not be going away just yet.

The post-war period did produce some good things. Some of the early boat trains had developed into the great 'named trains' – the *Golden Arrow* becoming a household name. The 1930s brought in the electrified *Brighton Belle*. Named trains and a period of streamlining raised the bar for all the railway companies throughout the 20s and 30s. The *Golden Arrow* became Victoria's flagship, and was later be hauled by one of Bulleid's Merchant

Navy class locos. An abiding image of Victoria is this Pullman train leaving the station headed by this classic engine, bearing all the regalia on the front.

During World War II exactly the same thing happened as during World War I. Massive damage and disruption was experienced and the government stepped in once again. This time nationalisation was taken up as the solution. On 1 January 1948, the Southern Region was created. The mighty SR had lasted just twenty-five years.

By this time nobody was too worried if all the signage wasn't changed, after all, the initials 'SR' also suited the new regime. The formation of the station was to stay the same. Upgrading would be done in an orderly fashion with severely limited funds being available from the cash-strapped government. Amazingly though, they did go for a programme of building a new set of twelve classes of steam engines, known as Standard classes. The old SR was still well short of having its system fully electrified, and a total of 999 new locomotives were built. This is remarkable, because in 1955 a plan was laid out to scrap all of them! Steam was to end within a decade.

The life of a station is therefore constantly changing due to the effects of history. Victoria still stands in its attractive Edwardian form. Those early planners, even allowing for two companies jostling over the same tracks, really did leave us with something worthwhile.

Once with the lettering BOAC proudly displayed at the top of the tower on four sides, this 1930s Art Deco airline terminal was a favourite backdrop for any photographer catching pictures of trains leaving Victoria Station. With the Victoria Coach Station opposite in Buckingham Palace Road, this area of West London was a great example of transport cooperation.

A steam hauled Pullman train heads off across the Thames to give its customers a circular tour around Surrey. After appreciating a fine meal in the classic surroundings of yesteryear, passengers are returned to Victoria. The iconic Battersea Power Station, formerly coal fired, stands right on the river.

This is the LC&DR side of Victoria Station. It was known as the 'Chatham' side until the amalgamations of 1923 brought the two sides together. It was first opened in 1860 and rebuilt to this form in 1908 with the dividing inner wall breached. This side had the boat train traffic and, thankfully, avoided losing the classic arched roof.

This view shows the bridging over at the back of the station for taxi and trade vehicle use. The image shows the half of the station that has been built over. In 1899 the LC&DR merged with its rival the SER, but the LB&SCR stayed separate until 1923, using the built-over side.

Above: In the corridor on the 'Brighton' side of the station, two tiled map displays are sited in recesses. These originate from the 1907 rebuilding of this side of the station. One shows the suburban system of the time and the other the LB&SCR network of lines from the station.

Opposite above: This is the LB&SCR side of Victoria Station, first opened in 1860 and rebuilt to this form in 1908. It was known as the 'Brighton' side until the amalgamations of 1923. The Grosvenor Hotel (on the right) was built at the same time as the station, but like all hotels of the period has been refitted along the way.

Opposite below: The 'Brighton' station building differed from its neighbour – the 'Chatham' side – in that it was largely built from brickwork as against the stone preferred by the SE&CR. Stone embellishments fitted the bill, with the clock being the focal point. The rivalry of the two occupiers of the station was intense, but they did have to share trackwork beyond the station.

Above: The most famous of the SR's steam hauled named trains was this, the 'Golden Arrow'. It came into being in the late 1920s and lasted right through into the days of BR. The service faded out during the war years, but on resumption one of Oliver Bulleid's air-smoothed Merchant Navy Class would take the service to Dover. One of these locomotives with full regalia is here hauling a chartered service past Olympia in West London.

Opposite above: On the Brighton side of the station it is very open and airy on the concourse. Once through into the platforms though, we find a building above us. That is often the cost of station development.

Opposite below: The 1923 amalgamations (which were a simplifying of railway affairs after the effects of World War I), brought it all together. The huge openings in the horrid, blank separating wall indicate there was much relish and joy in finally bringing the station into one ownership. Those warring private companies were something of the past. The station has operated very nicely ever since. Note the differing roof styles.

Departing from the station the train immediately encounters this busy stretch of trackwork before crossing the River Thames to pass the iconic Battersea Power Station. The Southern system has had third rail electrification here since 1931, after which steam and electric trains ran side by side until steam ended here in 1964. *Clan Line*, seen here taking out the 'Belmond British Pullman' lunchtime timetabled service, nicely recreates a lost scene.

The names of the Merchant Navy Class locos were added after the end of World War II. They commemorate the shipping lines which were involved in the Battle of the Atlantic and whose ships used Southampton docks. *Clan Line* was purchased privately after steam ended and therefore didn't end up being reduced to scrap.

Merchant Navy Class No. 35028 *Clan Line* powers up ready to depart with a lunchtime tour around Surrey with a British Pullman train. The diners are treated to the type of service that first class passengers had on the boat trains and continental services such as the Orient Express. The time of departure is 12.28.

Jigsaw-puzzle makers loved the Golden Arrow express train (which travelled to Paris via a ferry ride from Dover). A favourite puzzle was an image of the train passing the Art Deco BOAC terminal just outside the station. Here in all its regalia, the classic named train prepares to leave Victoria.

The SR was only in existence for 25 years from 1923 when 123 private companies were amalgamated into just four main regional companies. All signage then had to change. After nationalisation in 1948 it all changed again, with the SR becoming the Southern Region. However, just like the GWR, where the signage was set in stone, nobody had the inclination to change it. The Southern Region was unlikely to last long – and it didn't.

Wherever a generous arch like this can be seen on any station, it tells us that road traffic once ran through it. This roadway took taxis and goods vans through to Platform 3, into which the distinguished 'Golden Arrow' train ran.

This 1927 photograph shows buses on the forecourt where they have been found throughout the station's history. The speed limit at that time for buses with solid tyres was 12mph. The drivers were in the open but luckily for the top-deck passengers there was a roof. Note the number 38. This service, like some other numbers, still runs today.

Rebuilt in 1906 as a fine example of railway architecture, the 'Chatham' side of the station could cope with ever increasing usage. Also, this side had all the continental traffic, taking over as main operator from Charing Cross. Still with a foot in the door were the GWR as well as other south-eastern companies. This station forecourt is a prime example of how stations have to adapt to the changing times.

Above: The ever-present number 38 prepares to make its journey through Piccadilly, Shaftesbury Avenue and onwards. This has always been the best bus forecourt to any station in London. From the horse-drawn vehicles of a hundred years ago to today, the passengers transfer with ease.

Opposite above: A tourist bus sits next to the visitor centre with a taxi discharge point close by. The generous space at the front offers ongoing possibilities for little changes. The historical legacy of there being two different stations, occupied by two different companies, remains. The rivalry was so intense that they even tried to avoid building side by side. Now that bothers nobody as people go about their journeys.

Opposite below: An outside view of the former vehicle arch which is very convenient for passing out of the station. The designers on this side went for a Baroque style of building which was very popular at the turn of the twentieth century. Decoration was the thing, much to the chagrin of the modernists, who came later with their square boxes. On the left is the new Crossrail entrance.

An Edwardian postcard view of the open platform on the east side of the station. Commerce was as important then as it is now. The people in the picture stand stock still as a generation had to in those earlier days of slow-exposure photography. The high arched roof survived while those on the other side of the station didn't. It is always more pleasurable to begin a journey from a classic station rather than one overcome by redevelopers.

The LB&SCR Marsh H2 Atlantic (4-4-2 wheel arrangement) brings in a Brighton fast train to the 'Brighton' side of Victoria.

The LB&SCR crest shows the arms of London with Brighton at the bottom. To the sides are the extremities of the railway, Portsmouth and Hastings.

The cream of Southern steam would pull the flagship 'Golden Arrow' service. It is 11am and Merchant Navy Class 4-6-2 No. 35027 leads the Pullman train around the curve out of Victoria. The blue livery was used between 1949 and 1951. After nationalisation of the railways in 1948, the SR became the Southern Region of BR.

Britannia Class locomotive No. 70004 *William Shakespeare* waits at Victoria before taking a turn with the classic 'Golden Arrow.' This engine was on display at the 1951 Festival of Britain where it was housed in raised temporary accommodation over the southernmost lines between Waterloo East and Hungerford Bridge. This author remembers seeing it on display, turned out in a special livery.

CHAPTER 8

KING'S CROSS

K ing's Cross was always superior to its near neighbour, St Pancras, for it was the base of the East
Coast Main Line with all those great trains running to Scotland. St Pancras was always looked upon as
the 'monster next door'; a monstrosity covered in soot.

King's Cross, although simple in design, did fit its
purpose. Anyone looking at the front elevation would
immediately realise that it is a railway station – that is
good design. Lewis Cubitt had designed it well, and it is
easy to look at and an image that stays with you.

The double-barrelled train shed behind the façade is
a further wonder of station architecture. Unfortunately
for generations gone by, they never saw it at its best.
Once that soot and grime had taken hold, it would be
impossible to remove while those steam trains were running. But how we loved them! That is certainly proved
by the heritage movement which has evolved since the
'end of steam' in 1968.

The station was built on a tight site having had to
tunnel below the high ground immediately beyond the
platforms. This left a challenging approach area. If we
look at the new Euston and its passenger hall, the space
before the barriers at King's Cross was about a quarter
of that depth. Passengers had to view the arrivals and
departures board (on the east side wall) and *then* find
their way to the trains. The ticket office was off to the
side adjacent to the open Platform 10 (now 8). To com-
pound all this there was always a heavily laden cart train
weaving its way across the front area from the goods
side to unload its burden somewhere else, the little driver's unit constantly sounding its distinctive siren hooter.
To the right side as we look from the front, the main line
arrivals came in to discharge their passengers to the taxis
which crossed immediately to the front or to the buses in
York Way. The stairs to the Piccadilly and Metropolitan
Underground lines were also there, as they still are
today. Medium-range trains used the middle lines with
the left-hand side given over to long-distance departures. Suburban services had their own shed to the west
side which is still in use today. The 'hotel curve' brought
steam driven northbound trains from Moorgate around
and up among the suburban platforms. The engine and

train would come to a stop at the platform, still on the
slope. The smoke billowing from an N2 tank engine per-
forming the task of the climb followed by the stop and
start was something which once seen would never be
forgotten. This is one of the things the author saw as a
boy, standing at the end of Platform 10 (8) in the 1950s.
Health and safety wasn't given a thought back then.

Once a main line train had finished its unloading, an
N2 would take the carriages away and through the tunnels. The loco would then back out and shunt its way
across to the engine turning and coaling area to the left-
hand side. Trains constantly came and went from the
station and there was endless shunting going on in the
throat area. The big engines passed across the top of
Platform 10 (8), coming and going from their servicing.
A community of boy trainspotters would be taking it all
in and recording the numbers in their Ian Allen spotter's
books. Unbelievable theatre, and all free.

In the early days, King's Cross was obliged to allow
its rival, the Midland Railway (MR) to use the station, grudgingly to say the least. For fifteen years the
Great Northern Railway (GNR) charged a toll for this
use which started at three pence on every ticket sold.
Certainly a stiff penalty in those days, for which the
Midland looked to get revenge.

King's Cross always had the upper hand because it
was the starting point of the East Coast Main Line run
to Scotland. Euston became its rival with the West Coast
Main Line. It was a classic set up, which came to its first
head the 1890s with the races to the North. Both stations
would have their express depart at the same time to see
who got to Glasgow (West) and Edinburgh (East) first.
But that was not the end of it, for they would then race on
to Aberdeen. There was a squeeze at the end, when only
one could get onto the single-line approach to Aberdeen
Station. Therefore, whoever passed Kinnaber Junction,
thirty-eight miles short of Aberdeen, couldn't be beaten.
For King's Cross the journey time from London to
Edinburgh was reduced from ten hours in 1869 to six
and a half, managed by the 'Elizabethan' in 1955.

The racing subsided but the rivalry re-emerged in the
late 1920s and early 30s. King's Cross was host to some

of the greatest locos and named expresses running in the country. In those halcyon days the *Flying Scotsman* became the first engine to officially break the 100mph barrier. Then Nigel Gresley, the chief mechanical engineer, oversaw the design of the great streamlined A4s, and No. 4468 *Mallard* broke the all-time speed record in 1938 by reaching 126mph. Coming and going were all those great 'A Class' engines with their named trains hauling teak-bodied coaches to and from the station. All reviving that competitive spirit with their rivals, to great publicity.

Opposite above: The hotch-potch of buildings which had filled this space have now thankfully been removed. The front elevation of King's Cross Station has the special beauty of a design which shows the function of a building without the adornment of any unnecessary decoration. Even the large lettering has gone. The station never had an adequate concourse inside the building, which eventually led to the new facility on the west side. For a century taxis discharged passengers at the front between the 'village' and the station front. LNER offices were to the left with the goods depot on the right.

Opposite below: A view from Platform 8 (formerly 10) which has free access along its full length. Boy watchers (including this author) used this constantly in the 1950s and early 60s, the heyday of trainspotting. Back then at 10pm the Night Mail would leave this platform with its final destination being shown as Fort William. Along the way it would pick up and discharge pouches of mail.

LNER franchise services come into the former arrivals side of the station. All those great 'A' Class engines designed by Sir Nigel Gresley pulled in here with their trains coming off the East Coast Main Line. Carriages were often the Gresley teak-bodied type. All manner of porters and parcel carts would be milling around. Whistles, hooters, loudspeakers and hissing steam filled the place with noise. Those stove-enamel advertising signs adorned the walls where they had been untouched since that style was invented in the late 1890s. It was just a few steps across the concourse to where the taxis pulled in.

There is a downward slope of 1 in 100 from the station to halfway through the tunnel where the lines rise sharply at 1 in 107. This gave the engine crews a good run at the incline. Although the Regent's Canal passes over the top, there is no record of this being a 'wet' tunnel. The turntable and coaling tower were to the left. The steam locos would have to shunt over, between gaps in the comings and goings of suburban and main line rail traffic. This area was one of the best viewing points for steam action anywhere in the country. Due to the reorganisations, the right-hand tunnel is now no longer used. Over that side was a station called York Way, once connected with the Underground lines.

A look northwards from the raised walkway halfway down the platform on the former departures side – Platforms 5 to 8. The slickness and efficiency of electric trains enables all platforms now to be for arrivals and departures. The days of uncoupling and turning steam and diesel locos are long gone.

The north end of the station reveals the vertical glazing which matches that of the front. The double barrel-vault roof is a classic. Formerly, a footbridge halfway down the station would block the continuous view of the shed. The lighter crossing now installed gives us a pure view of the structure. For modern-day spotters the train in the platform is clearly seen as Class 700 No. 700110.

The access staircase to the new cross-walk from the platforms leads to the new concourse on the west side of the station. The former footbridge, which came with the station in 1852, never proved practical, therefore it was continuously closed off from the platforms. It survived as a connection for the offices on the east side with those on the west. 'Platform 0' is a new line added to what was previously the cab road and later a goods vehicle access. Note the blue brick pier protection.

The bright, new and long awaited booking hall and concourse. Previously, passengers had to cram into the tight spaces provided within the original station. Passages lead to the main line station below the offices and former booking hall on the right. The west-side suburban arrival and departure train shed leads off from the far end. A statue of Sir Nigel Gresley is a centrepiece to the space, sited below the string of offices which were the company headquarters.

The hotel is a survivor; where others failed it kept going. There are two side sections, both straight with the centre part making the curve. The curve followed the old road-line of Pancras Way. A curving and climbing rail line passes below the hotel connecting the Metropolitan Railway with the King's Cross main and suburban lines. This was a horrendous and dangerous line – long since closed. For the first time the hotel is connected to the main station with the addition of the new concourse extension.

Two names which will always be part of King's Cross and will never be allowed to die. The GNR and the LNER both at one time had their names emblazoned across the top of the station frontage. After the Grouping of 1923 the LNER took over from the GNR, followed by BR in 1948, when the railways were nationalised. In the 1990s privatisation returned, and those great old titles were reinstated as the chosen names of franchise companies.

Above: A1950s picture of the old station with an assortment of shops and businesses taking up the space in front of it. York Way is to the right, where many bus routes terminated to discharge their passengers. Taxis came across the front of the building from the left under the roof just in front of the station. That 'village' has now been taken away, which was a brave bit of replanning.

Opposite above: The Great Northern Hotel of King's Cross sits in the shadow of its noisy neighbour. This hotel survived while the St Pancras Hotel closed in 1933. Its curved shape once followed a sub-surface branch but now handily gives a profile to the new booking office and concourse. With station replanning it is nearly always the case that taxis have to take a new route. Now the taxi point for both stations is here in one place.

Opposite below: Sitting proudly in the National Railway Museum is the most famous engine of all. A regular for the East Coast run to and from Scotland, it was just before Peterborough where it broke the world steam speed record, achieving 126mph on 3 July 1938.

AFTERNOON DEPARTURES FROM KINGS CROSS IN THE LATE 1920s
Gresley 'A1' Pacifics 2551 *Prince Palatine* and 2567 *Sir Visto* with down expresses;
in the centre, on No 9 carriage road (removed in 1938), Great Northern 'C1' Atlantic
No 4417

Above: Pleased to be back, heading up the East Coast Main Line after undergoing a ten-year overhaul, A3 4-6-2 (Pacific) No. 60103 *Flying Scotsman* passes Conington on a north-bound inaugural run. The engine was the first to officially break the 100mph barrier and also power the first non-stop run between King's Cross and Edinburgh Waverley in 1928.

Opposite: Painting by artist V. Welch of 1926. Depicted is an early evening scene at Kings Cross in the late 1920s. Nigel Gresley's 'A1' Pacifics (4-6-2 wheel arrangements) are to the outside. No. 2551 *Prince Palatine* and No. 2567 *Sir Visto* with GNR 'C1' Atlantic (4-4-2 wheel arrangement) No. 4417 in the holding road. This track was removed in 1938 with platform re-arrangements.

Designed for suburban and shunting duties around King's Cross, the class also had to provide the motive power to go underground to join the Metropolitan lines through to Moorgate. Hence the condensing apparatus fitted to the sides. Of a class numbering 107 at the time of nationalisation in 1948, this is the only survivor. Built in 1921 before the time of railway Grouping, N2 0-6-2T No. 1744 is seen here in the GNR livery of the time, enjoying retirement on the North Norfolk Railway.

A steam engine backs onto a train at King's Cross Station. The engine in the picture is the former Southern Region West Country Class No. 34046 *Braunton* which is substituting for LNER A4 No. 60009 *Union of South Africa*. On this occasion the streamliner had to pull out because of technical problems.

D9016 *Gordon Highlander* and D9000 *Royal Scots Grey* are two of the six surviving Deltic diesel engines, originally a class of just 22 designed for the East Coast Main Line. These two are celebrating their fiftieth birthday at the East Lancs Railway. They were built and adapted by the English Electric Company using engines first designed for naval minesweepers. Both of these locomotives are active on British preserved lines and are seen here at Rawtenstall on the East Lancs Railway.

Powerful steam engines were replaced by the big diesel/electric locos. Deltics had two triangular engines, each with six pistons working in unison, providing the power. These in turn powered an electric generator which powered the wheels. No more of the three-hour building up of steam was needed with these. Not much more than pressing a button. Drivers liked them except for one thing – the noise. When powering along at 100mph the sounds were deafening. This was alleviated somewhat with modifications. This is Deltic No. 55005 the *Prince of Wales' Own Regiment of Yorkshire*.

The 'village' to the left blocks out the station frontage. A canopy has been completed for taxis to pick up and put down passengers at the front of the station. Previously there was a cab road was underneath the goods offices to the right of the picture. Platform 0 now occupies this area. An iron footbridge was installed across the middle of the station to connect the extended offices with the main offices to the west side. Although the footbridge connected to the platforms, it was never successfully used by passengers. Note the tramlines in the road.

L.N.E.R. "SILVER LINK" ENGINE
PULLING THE "SILVER JUBILEE" TRAIN AT KING'S CROSS STATION

By the mid-1930s, the mania for publicity led to a new era – streamlining. Nigel Gresley took this up with the introduction of the classic A4 Pacifics. To mark the Silver Jubilee of King George V, A4 No. 2509 *Silver Link*, together with her train, were painted silver to celebrate the occasion. It did the trick, for here at King's Cross the departure on the 29 September 1935 created huge interest.

Gresley Pacific A1/3 No. 2561 (BR 60062) *Minori* heads an express from King's Cross c. 1935. The train is about to enter Gasworks Tunnel before heading northwards along the East Coast Main Line. Again, pride in appearance is apparent through this period.

Also c. 1935 a J52 0-6-0 saddle tank heads a goods train past the York Road platform which adjoined King's Cross station on the east side. Heading southward, the train is about to descend to join the tunnels of the Metropolitan Line. Heading to Farringdon, the train can turn southward and be banked up two levels to cross the Thames at Blackfriars. The route always kept going for freight but from 1908 was not maintained for passenger traffic. A Moorgate-bound steam hauled passenger service did however keep going until the 1950s.

CHAPTER 9

ST PANCRAS

By the mid-nineteenth century MR had become the largest railway company in the country. Founded by one of the four biggest rail entrepreneurs of the nineteenth century, George Hudson, there was now the overwhelming desire for the company to have its own London terminus.

For fifteen years, from 1853 to 1868 the MR had lodged with it neighbour at King's Cross, the Great Northern Railway (GNR). The GNR had generally treated the MR pretty badly, so it was no surprise that when the chance came to become bigger and better, it was quickly taken: any opportunity to be able to finally look down on the GNR (quite literally).

The site selected was just across the road, and with the Regent's Canal crossing the path of the railway just a quarter of a mile out, the MR would have to bridge over it. This meant that as a starting point the new station would have a starting level one storey above that of the MR's rival. The company was not going to miss this chance to overwhelm its disliked neighbour, and Sir George Gilbert Scott was selected to be the architect; he loved the high and mighty Gothic style, having designed the Albert Memorial in Hyde Park.

Scott was to design the showpiece hotel for the front elevation. But firstly the task of designing the station building was given to engineer William Barlow.

A better choice could not have been made, for the finished article became the largest single-spanned roof in the world. It stayed such until way into the next century. The steel for the structure came from the Butterley works in Derbyshire – right in the heart of Midland country, for the MR always keep its headquarters at Derby. Barlow didn't make the arch a pure semicircle, he put in a ridge, perhaps to enable him to make the structure higher and wider (plus a bit Gothic). It was completed in 1868 when the station opened for business.

There had been a few problems in acquiring the land outside the station. A whole churchyard had to be uprooted, with thousands of bodies reinterred at a new graveyard in North London. Also, approaching 4,000 people were evicted from their homes in Somers Town and Agar Town. With the government showing minimum interest in the welfare of the local inhabitants, companies could do such things in those days. The MR for its part also showed minimum interest. The outcome was that existing slum communities immediately had their housing densities increased. As the century wore on, governments did eventually ensure that persons displaced by rail expansion had to be rehoused by the appropriate company.

The hotel was duly completed in 1873 whereby it became the finest in London. The facilities included elevators, or 'rising rooms' as they were called then. At its raised level the access given to vehicles was excellent with a rising grade road leading to a large throughway to the station and a discharge point at the top.

The building was superb, with bright-red coloured brickwork set off by white stonework. Throughout the inside, individual carvings were applied to the capitals and full thought was given to every aspect. For all this glory, the MR never matched its rivals at Euston or King's Cross in dominating the best routes in the country. It did get to Scotland, but this was by the route through Nottingham and the Settle to Carlisle line. Hence the railway was always appearing to go down while its rivals led an upward path. Even the hotel struggled, leading the way at the start, but the bathroom facilities proved to be inadequate, which in the end led to its closure in 1933.

The appearance of the building also suffered in a smoke-filled city. All its colours became obscured, which left it standing as an eyesore. Very few people could see good in it. Against it was also an architectural 'modernist' revival leaving a desire among designers to avoid redecoration at all costs.

The MR never built the largest of locomotives. It was its policy to just double up when a train needed to be longer or heavier. This policy carried on right through the Grouping of 1923 when all the private companies (over 120 of them) were rationalised into just four. This was a government-led initiative owing to the dilapidated state of the system after World War I. After the second conflict, the railway system became nationalised, in 1948.

After 1923, St Pancras was part of the London Midland and Scottish Railway (LMS). Yet, even then, no larger locos were built. The doubling up continued as needed. In the 1930s it was Euston (also part of the LMS) that got the larger engines. St Pancras had to persevere with medium-sized engines such as the Jubilees and the Black 5s.

After 2007, the station became known as St Pancras International when the big extensions we see today were opened by the Queen. The medium-range domestic services to Sheffield, Derby and Nottingham still run, but it is now all about those high speed trains to the Continent.

The tall and imposing Gothic station of St Pancras stands proud in the summer sunshine. Its near neighbour, King's Cross sits well in the distance but at a lower level. For a century St Pancras was covered in the London smoke dust – black and ugly. Only a few people could see any beauty or take pleasure from the former hotel building and for a long time it was destined to go. The loss of the Euston Arch may have been its saviour, for at the time, following the loss, a movement emerged to save old buildings.

A lover of Victorian architecture, Sir John Betjeman (1906–1984) had been part of a spirited push to save the Euston Arch – but he failed. He was the founder of the Victorian Society and full of enthusiasm to try and save nineteenth-century buildings which had fallen out of favour. Betjeman and his friends and followers led a vigorous campaign for the hotel and in this case were successful. BR wanted the hotel demolished and it's anyone's guess what they would have replaced it with. The statue by Martin Jennings is a lasting tribute to this popular poet.

Opposite above: The Eurostar trains from Paris and Brussels have arrived – now waiting to make the return trip. Two and a half hours to Paris, city centre to city centre, is quite impressive. The long train extends past the end screen into the new extension at the far end. The whole station had to be completely re-planned for it to work. On the left are escalator connections to the lower areas. It can be seen that the roof is not a semi-circle as it comes to a point at the apex.

Opposite below: At the far end of the old station the screen connects with the new flat roofed extension. The international trains share this area with the arrivals and departures of trains to destinations in this country. The glazing to the roof and its infrastructure are all to modern standards. William Barlow's original roof structure has been retained and improved: much of Barlow's original cast iron has been replaced by steel, but it is of course still Barlow's shed.

The hotel end of the station as it was before the Eurostar upgrading. The end screen protected the hotel from the station smoke. There was a tired look to everything as decades passed with there not being the will or finance to do anything except essential maintenance work. The hotel (or since 1934 offices), became unused with the train shed remaining grubby and unimpressive. There was some wartime bomb damage which led to overhauling. But it was all just sitting there waiting for something to happen.

Whoever made the decision to transfer the Eurostar services to the north-facing St Pancras must have had good vision. It was what the station had been waiting for – a new purpose with massive government involvement. The result is here for us to see and marvel at. Hardly a bad word could be said as the old place goes forward with pride.

With its new concourse using the former Burton-on-Trent beer storage area, Eurostar's new St Pancras International had little option other than to use the former horse and dray's entrance onto Pancras Road. All now wonderfully upgraded, the area links well with the King's Cross concourse and taxi area across the road. St Pancras Station was designed with platforms at the higher level. This enabled the outgoing lines to bridge over the existing roads and Regent's Canal.

The former brewery undercroft just through from the street entrance now looks nothing like it once did. After the brewery departed the area was split up for use by small businesses. This area now provides all the passenger services needed before they move to the level above to board the trains. The columns are cast iron mouldings. The shelf brackets never had any function, although they now give a uniqueness to this station and its famous undercroft.

Above: From Pentonville Road: this painting of 1884 by John O'Connor, more than anything, shows St Pancras Station as the owners wanted it to be: high and uplifting to show up its neighbour King's Cross. The MR had to share King's Cross for fifteen years before it was able to get its own facility – and how the company hated its time there. The owners of the GNR treated the MR shabbily and from 1868 it was their turn to be superior. The Gothic style with all those uplifting pinnacles was the chosen design. This painting makes no excuse for rubbing it all in.

The former booking office before it was all taken downstairs. It was conveniently located with an exit straight onto the concourse area. High craftsmanship went into constructing the wooden screening. Now this area is a smart restaurant where some of the timber panels have been incorporated into the interior. It originally had a high ceiling, and BR put in a lower flat ceiling with downlighting.

St Pancras never had the top LMS locomotives. The Coronations, Duchesses and Princesses went to Euston for the top-link runs to Glasgow over the West Coast Main Line. This station did have services to Scotland at one time via the Settle to Carlisle line. But generally it was the mid-range distances which were served from here. Nottingham, Sheffield, Derby etc. were, and still are, the staple routes. The lesser powered locomotives served these, sometimes doubling up for an especially heavy train. The top picture shows a Black 5 – probably the finest general purpose engine this country has ever produced. This one, seen at the North York Moors preserved railway, is number 45212 built at the Armstrong Whitworth works in 1935. Below, the picture shows a Jubilee. No. 5593 *Kolaphur*, built at the North British works in Glasgow in 1934 and here seen resplendent in Midland Red livery at Tyseley Locomotive Works, Birmingham.

Rising on the escalator from the undercroft, the full wonder of Barlow's shed can be appreciated. When built it was the largest single span of any building in the world. The mighty station is now shown off in all its glory. Betjeman would surely have approved. The lower area has shops and outlets to suit those in a hurry, while upstairs the food and drink areas are for those with a little more time.

With the fast turnaround that modern trains can make, only four platforms at St Pancras are enough to cope with the short- and long-haul domestic routes. Class 222, along with most of the current modern trains, has a life expectancy of thirty to thirty-five years, although the levels of comfort can be a little underwhelming. No. 222002 is about to take out a train bound for Sheffield.

Entrance after the Eurostar modernisation.

Goods vehicle entrance before Eurostar, with the gasworks visible in the distance.

Side entrance onto Pancras Road in the 1990s.

Above: The Butterley Company sign their work in 1867.

Left: Undercroft before restoration.

Roof in 1998 before restoration works.

Above: The eighteen-coach Eurostar train takes up the whole length of the new St Pancras station, with the domestic 437 being just about half that length. The HSTs had an incredible 40+-year life but have now been phased out. St Pancras, as well as Paddington and King's Cross, has had the benefit of these marvellous trains. No. 43480 carries the name *Valenta 1972–2010* to commemorate the superb Paxman diesel engines which produce the power.

Right: Just a thin wire fence defines the boundary between the two railway operators. In days gone by this would have been a substantial masonry wall. Once leaving the station, the train will bear to the right to pass underground for four miles before reaching Stratford, the huge multi-interchange in the east of London.

Always a target for the Luftwaffe, most leading stations caught at least one bomb. Here at St Pancras it came in 1940.

Left and opposite above: Details from the sculptured frieze at the base of Paul Day's *Lovers* statue.

Part of the original capital sculptures inside the goods vehicle entrance.

CHAPTER 10

MARYLEBONE

Marylebone was the last of the London termini to be built in Victorian times, that great period of railway expansion. It opened in 1899 as a very unassuming railway station in a quiet and salubrious part of the capital. Its early history centred around one man, Edward Watkin, and what was to become his Great Central Railway (GCR).

Watkin was chairman of the Manchester, Sheffield & Lincolnshire Railway (MS&LR), a northern company obviously operating a long way from London. But he wanted to get to the capital and beyond, and he was a very ambitious man. Being a Manchester mill owner, he, like most of his contemporaries, had become most enamoured of railway expansion. The business opportunities shone out as did the possibilities of fame and fortune. His dream was to have no boundaries, and once he came south he wanted to go further, to the Continent. He became chairman of the MS&LR in 1864 and spent the next thirty years pursuing his dream. By buying up small companies and amalgamating with others, he got his line south but only as far as Quainton Road in Buckinghamshire. This line came southward from Sheffield, Nottingham, Loughborough, Leicester and so on. Therefore it was almost duplicating the service running into St Pancras.

To further his ambitions Sir Edward, as he had become, had also worked his way onto the board of the Metropolitan Railway to become their chairman in 1872. The Met had lines coming into the heart of the capital, and had opened the first Underground line ever between Farringdon and Paddington. This later expanded northward beyond Baker Street and as far as Harrow. The Met also connected with Blackfriars and the line across the Thames.

Sir Edward was getting on a bit by the 1890s, but had acquired running rights with the Metropolitan and had doubled its lines to run a fast service bypassing many stations between Harrow and Finchley Road. Now having a partner in the Met to help with putting proposals before Parliament, he proposed the branching and creation of a new line at Finchley Road to divert south, passing through the east side of Lord's cricket ground to Marylebone Road.

Obviously there were many objectors as the line had to be tunnelled using mostly the 'cut-and-fill' method, the system which had been used by the Met for the full lengths of Euston and Marylebone Roads. Lord's was particularly vociferous in its objections, as this scheme would mean the cutting through its secondary pitch on the easterly side of the ground. Never mind, it all got agreed and passed. Sir Edward at this point decided to upgrade his combined railway and call it the 'Great Central Railway' in 1898.

A hotel was also deemed necessary for the new station, but with money running short the funding for this was passed to Sir Blundell Maple of the department store fame. A 700-room structure was built on the Marylebone Road, completely obscuring the new station from the main thoroughfare.

Watkin also had dreams of expanding even more southward into Kent and desired be part of the first ever scheme to build a Channel tunnel. To do this he would have had to get running rights across London. He got as far as joining the board of the SER, but that was as far as it went. However, he did have a London terminus which offered main line travel to Manchester. Very nice, but the main lines running from Euston and St Pancras also had similar running rights and they had got there first. Because of his declining health, Watkin employed a very capable manager in Samuel Fay to run the railway from its Marylebone base. With all that competition the one thing Fay could offer his travelling public was luxury. High quality furnishings together with buffet facilities took the railway where no others had been. But after these early flourishes the company went into a slow decline.

Throughout all those decades Marylebone was looked upon as an underused luxury which was surplus to requirements. Everybody made predictions about its closure. That is until the 1990s when Network South East suddenly took an interest in the possibilities. BR was still nationalised at this time but it was going to be in 1996 that it all went private.

The GCR was lost as far back as 1923 when the Grouping took place and the line came under the auspices of the LNER. The former GCR north of Aylesbury carried on until final closure in 1966. Marylebone's reputation was on the decline from that time, with the mundane Class 115 DMUs handling all suburban services until 1990. Network Rail's new initiatives brought in much improved rolling stock with plans to extend running services through to Oxford and Birmingham.

With privatisation everything improved dramatically. Marylebone offered the wealthy areas of north-west London a commuter service they would be pleased to use. Lines made connections with High Wycombe and took over the running on former Great Western routes with speeds available up to 100mph, but no electric running power. The new operator was Chiltern Railways.

Above: While always going to be concealed by the hotel, the station never aspired to be anything lavish at the front. The pink-brick building does have some cream stone embellishments with a few terracotta features. The former cab road now provides good pedestrian access with a glimpse of something more special inside.

Opposite above: The elegant canopy is a fine surprise to those walking round from Marylebone Road. The station was the last London terminus to be built before World War I, being opened in 1899. Sir Edward Watkin had extended the GCR here after obtaining running rights with the Metropolitan Railway of which he had become chairman.

Opposite below: Nowadays the station is well used and thriving. Seats are even provided for the passengers. The destination board shows that trains are soon to depart to Aylesbury, Oxford, Birmingham Snow Hill and Gerrards Cross. Tickets are available from the machines.

Above: The redevelopment of the station in 1991 was done with the underlying thought that the BR Board really wanted to make something of this station, with a seriously useful and dedicated future – and they succeeded. The western shed, on the right here, was removed, to allow an office building to take up half the platform lengths. This effectively financed the whole operation. Now with a refurbished double-span roof to the left, three lines is plenty for the long-distance trains. Not forgetting that these days the trains can be 'turned round' very quickly. The western shorter side copes very well with the shorter suburban trains.

Opposite above: At the same tine, and with the new office development encroaching into the station, all the shops and kiosks have been rebuilt in the style of the station. The glass and iron roofing has survived superbly to give us a terminus in the true London tradition.

Opposite below: So good and correct was the 1990's overhaul of Marylebone that its glory still shows today. People love to come and go from this station, which is clear to see, for they do have alternatives for those distant destinations. Even the selection of rolling stock was right in that the turbo-diesel 165s still run today. After railway privatisation in 1996, the new operator, Chiltern Railways, took over a fleet of 43 from BR, overhauled them in 2003, and they still run two decades later.

Left: The suburban side serves beyond the now over-built fields of Metroland, past Harrow on the Hill and into south Buckinghamshire. The very discerning public living in places like Rickmansworth, Chorleywood, Chalfont & Latimer and Amersham love their swift commute. It serves them very well.

Below: The Great Central Hotel was designed to be luxurious and lavish. But with the station proving to be under-used for the greater part of the last century, changes were inevitable. Like many of the station hotels it came under government control for both world wars. After World War II there was no going back. The nationalised railway executive took it over to be its London headquarters. Further railway changes through the next decades left it with nowhere to go. Until, that is, in the last decade of the century when Marylebone Station had a big uplift. This was reflected in the fortunes of the hotel when new owners took it over to resurrect it as a luxury establishment.

In its dark times the building was just known for its postal address – Number 222. No expense was spared, though, when it was designed. For this railway was aiming to introduce more luxurious travel than any of its rivals. With the hotel being effectively the station frontage to the world, the designers didn't hold back. Hence the carved eye-catching terracotta helmeted and scanty-clad females over the main entrance. The hotel has always obscured the station from the main road, but now the London plane trees are doing the same thing to the hotel.

Only two named trains ran from Marylebone. A show was made by the newly nationalised railways when the LNER became the Eastern Region in 1948. the 'Master Cutler' and the 'South Yorkshireman' ran to fairly relaxed timetables. This though was during the times of the railway's decline and they finished in 1960.

LONDON AND NORTH EASTERN RLY.

After 1923 railway companies were grouped into just four. Marylebone came under the auspices of the LNER. That company largely covered the eastern side of England and history shows that it didn't really want this line. The former GCR was always in rivalry with the MR, both of which ran to Nottingham and beyond. If one were to go it would be the GCR – and it did, in 1966. But the LNER had to make something of it, as depicted in this postcard, showing loco 4-6-0 No. 423 when there was still some pride in an engine's appearance.

CHAPTER 11

PADDINGTON

Built in a slight dip, Paddington has no particular front elevation. On Praed Street there is the Great Western Hotel and the south-west side is taken up with company offices, adjoining Eastbourne Terrace.

However, if we go down one of the slopes and pass into the station we enter one of the great station spaces in the world. Unlike St Pancras, which has one shed, or King's Cross, which has two, Paddington was built with three and extended to four. The design is so good that there is brilliant visibility across all of them.

Brunel, with the help of his associates, Wyatt and others, came up with a palace, or cathedral, if you like, in terms of the design. This was in part inspired by Paxton's Crystal Palace, the construction of which had shown what could be produced from iron and glass. This was the GWR and new technology was always welcome. So the same contractors who had built the Crystal Palace built Paddington Station.

The arches are not semicircular but take the shape of an ellipse cut in half. The end screens are adorned with pre-Art Noveau swirling curlicues, which give them a bit of what we might now call a 'Parisian touch'. Along the shed (we shouldn't really call it that) in two locations are the roof breaks, with visual cross-entry points – transepts.

At Brunel's original Bristol terminus – a timber building which still exists – four tracks came into one space with little turntables incorporated into its length. This allowed the switching and marshalling of wagons into different formations within the station. This was also done initially at Paddington but the station could only accommodate the early period small carriages. Once demand increased and trains became longer, all the space within each shed was taken up with additional platforms. Those cross-breaks through the transepts were an early idea to pick up a carriage like a container, turn it and then place it within a train in the next area. In the early days carriage sidings away from the station hadn't come into the planning process.

Brunel's station was opened in 1855 with just one set of tracks on the approach lines. This was quadrupled in the late 1870s.

A specialist, Owen Jones, had been brought in to provide the colour scheme, only for it to disappear within a couple of years under soot. Paddington, though, was one of the great stations which could still have been appreciated in its blackened form. Those great wide spaces in which the traveller-admirer could walk can still be appreciated. Unlike, say, Liverpool Street and Waterloo, the barrier areas are kept clear and uncluttered, leaving great views.

The Lawn, which was never a lawn, just a hard concourse, took its name from a grassed area at the back of the hotel site. But the name continued as it still does, and one hopes always will do. The swirling artistic feature here was installed during the station remodelling, which was completed in 1935. The extensions, which included an additional shed being added, were completed in 1916, following a decade of planning and improvements following the electrification of the Metropolitan connection in 1906.

Paddington Timeline

1835	GWR Act passed by Parliament giving permission to build a railway between London and Bristol.
1838	Temporary station built and opened at Bishop's Bridge Road just to the north-west of the present site, adjacent to the canal. A service ran from here to Maidenhead Riverside (the bridge wasn't ready yet).
1841	The GWR opens the London to Bristol line.
1842	13 June. Queen Victoria makes her first railway journey between Slough and Paddington.
1854	29 May. The new Paddington Station is opened, followed by the opening of the Great Western Hotel (designed by Philip Hardwicke, who also designed the Euston Arch).
1860	William Powell Frith completes his painting *The Railway Station*.

1861	Paddington Station is fitted with mixed-gauge trackwork.
1892	End of broad gauge. The last train on the 7' wide lines runs on 20 May.
1913–1915	The station is enlarged with the opening of the fourth shed to the north-east side.
1922	11 November. The war memorial on Platform 1 is unveiled to commemorate the 3,312 GWR employees killed in the Great War. A scroll of names is kept in the base (in World War I railway work was not designated a 'reserved occupation').
1930–1935	The station is further enlarged and remodelled and platforms extended.
1965	11 June. Last timetabled steam-hauled train departs.
2009	Electrification of lines between Paddington and Swansea via Bristol is announced.
2011	14 July. Network Rail and the Department of Transport announce the introduction of a £5 billion programme of improvements for the main line.

Just like all the other major stations, Paddington has had its share of prestigious-named trains. The 'Bristolian' travelled the length of Brunel's original installed track. The 'Cheltenham Flyer' became the fastest recorded service for a time of any steam-hauled train. The 'Torbay Express' left Paddington daily with its destination being Kingswear, at what is now the preserved Paignton and Dartmouth Steam Railway. But the most famous was the 'Cornish Riviera Express' which left London daily at 10.30. This train travelled non-stop to Plymouth, a distance of over 230 miles. For this journey the fireman would be shovelling over two tons of coal into the firebox of the hungry King Class locomotive. These services carried on after the end of steam in this station, but they were never the same. Like the *Flying Scotsman* from King's Cross, the service faded to become a subheading in the timetable. The romance of it all went after the steam days.

In modern times, since the 1990s, electrification has been accompanied by services to Heathrow Airport being added. The InterCity 125s provided sterling service for nearly forty years, but in 2018 the last of these ran, giving way to the new breed of electric trains. The lines from Paddington all had the installation of overhead wires, whereby the trackbeds had to be lowered by some 600mm.

Now the station connects with the Crossrail service, bringing much improved connections to the City and the West End. It's also possible to now take in the station in all its beauty and wonderment, for, with all these improvements the chance has been taken to bring the station back to its original look, with all that ironwork now seeming as good as new.

The modern-day tower at the back of the station is typical of many locations in London. The 1930s Underground roundel sits over the 1960s BR logo, both of which have survived well as recognisable symbols of what they represent. Simple, bright and straightforward is what works well.

On Platform 1 just below the company boardroom sits the GWR's tribute to its 3,312 employees who gave their lives for their country in World War I. Designed by Charles Sargeant Jagger in bronze, it depicts a soldier reading a letter from home. It was dedicated on Armistice Day 1922.

The transepts – side access points to the iron archways – occur in two places along the station's length. Originally these cross-access points may have been thought to provide facility for the original small carriages of a train to be lifted by a pulley. These then would be taken crossways to make up a train in the adjoining section.

One of the final runs into Paddington for the highly successful HST 125s. From the early 1970s until May 2019 they worked superbly, bringing their high-speed capability to western services. With barely a cross word from any of the users, these trains gave the capability of long-distance commuting for those living in the West Country. With the region having partial overhead traction added, the 125s have been replaced by the bi-mode Azumas.

The overhead wires are barely visible to detract from the iron structure of the building. The view is of Platform 9 with the former taxi access ramp to the left. The taxis now use the east side of the station adjacent to the canal basin. Brunel's original station of 1855 consisted of three 'sheds' of which this one would have been on the left as seen from the platform ends.

Platform 1 has always been ungated with free access being available to station users. Originally the departure side of the station, the three-faced clock would always have been there as a meeting point. Ticket offices, left luggage and many other services used these areas with the access road being adjacent to Eastbourne Terrace. The clock has been electrically operated since 1929 with the stationmaster having control of the mechanism.

Brunel has ensured that the name of the GWR will last forever – even if it does have some tweaking along the way. Here the great man sits alongside his greatest creation, Paddington Station. Unlike cathedrals, great stations have to adapt to changing times. There are ongoing changes in technology and travelling styles which a station has to absorb. The great designs survive while others don't and have to be rebuilt.

The station had to be originally built below street level to ensure the lines going out are reasonably level. No problems here as Brunel's track was nicknamed the 'Billiard Table' all the way to Bristol, where he designed that station also. The picture shows the former taxi-way rising from below the 1910–1914 extension into Praed Street.

Adjoining Eastbourne Terrace, the slip road falls to station concourse level. This was the departing side and further along this road, goods vehicles would discharge packets etc. to the parcels depot. The side of the hotel and station offices are next to the service road. The sides of the buildings are typical of all buildings which started to be cleaned in the 1980s.

One of the classic Great Western locomotives is preparing to take a scheduled service out of the station. No. 5018 *St Mawes Castle* was one of the engine class which ran from the early 1920s until the end of steam here in 1964. The class was so successful that after the war new examples were being built at the same time as some of the originals were being scrapped. It can be seen that even in steam days the station had a good look to it.

Inspired by the Japanese bullet train, but with a shorter nose, the Azumas are fitted out at the Hitachi factory at Newton Aycliffe, Durham. The bodies are constructed in Japan. They are bi-mode, capable of being diesel powered or by the overhead power lines via the pantograph.

The technology of ninety years earlier has made a visit to Paddington: an A4 steam engine from the former Eastern Region of BR. A4 No. 60009 *Union of South Africa* waits to depart with a steam tour to take enthusiasts to the West Country and back. The similarity of the shape to the Azumas makes it very clear that the A4 designer, Sir Nigel Gresley was way ahead of his time, although he did get some input from an Italian designer also.

The destination board is tastefully located long-ways and easily read from the concourse. It is not shielding the views across the station. Fortunately the station was designed with generous circulating areas. From the concourse, the station can really be appreciated.

Around the barriers, passengers have wonderful views of the station structure. The eye quickly goes upwards to appreciate it. Because of this, there will always be the desire to keep it clean. It would not do to keep the sunlight out. After a decade of renovations, present generations are fortunate to see it at its best. Even the colouring of the panels has recreated the vision of the designers in the 1850s.

Above: The Kings were the all-time steam stars of the GWR, its most powerful and most prestigious class. So powerful were they that they ran just four routes. All the mighty named trains of the GWR such as the 'Cornish Riviera Express' always had a King to take them if available. No. 6023 King Edward II is here in the short-lived BR blue livery of 1949/1951. Now residing at the GWR working museum at Didcot.

Opposite above: A visitor who is attracting some very special attention. GWR Hall Class No. 5972 is well at home in her old running ground of Paddington. The engine found new fame as a star in the film *Harry Potter and the Philosopher's Stone*, and here the engine prepares to take out a train full of adoring fans.

Opposite below: The three arched roofs of the original Brunel station are still proudly on show here. On the left is a later addition built when the station was extended just before World War I. The station opened in 1854 when there were just two platforms below each section. Two siding tracks were additionally laid between these. The small carriages used at the time could be interchanged between tracks on little turntables.

All the major stations had a hotel constructed around the same time as the station. They had reason to be prestigious with top architects being chosen to design them. The GWR attempted to attract travellers to take their trains to such ports as Bristol, Weymouth, Plymouth or even Fishguard and then take their own ships onward to various destinations.

Matthew Wyatt was employed by Brunel to add some embellishments to his iron and glass structure. One of his contributions (as well as the decorative ends to the train sheds) was these oriel windows. This is the company's meeting room where, as well as Brunel, figures such as Gooch, Dean, Churchward and Collett would have attended. Note that the windows line up with one of the roof transepts.

This view shows how the platforms have been extended into the sharp curve out of the station. The end screens all have Matthew Wyatt's Art Nouveau style metal tracery embellishing them. In the background the 1930s tower of the hotel extension stands proud, still showing the GWR lettering which was never removed.

The former cab road now has a different use. Looking towards the buffer end of the station, the exit to Praed Street can be seen. This is the side of the station where the additional fourth large arch was added in 1913/1915. The columns and roof structure are made of steel, unlike the originals which are of wrought iron, although some have been replaced. Rainwater pipes run down inside the columns.

Above: Out on the north side of the station beyond the platforms of the Hammersmith & City line of London Underground, the station comes up against the spur of Regent's Canal. In former times this served the railway goods depot, but now this secretive little area offers the chance for some very relaxed wining and dining.

Opposite above: Heathrow Express 332002 awaits to depart Paddington with a fifteen-minute non-stop run to the airport. These fine electric trains have been providing the airport service for over twenty years – receiving very favourable feedback from users. Combinations of four or five carriage sets can be made up to meet demand.

Opposite below: Back to times gone by with a view of how things looked in the days of broad-gauge trackwork. Young and old are depicted in this print looking on in awe at the monster machine in front of them. Broad gauge finished in 1892, but for some thirty or forty years before this, dual-gauge working had been catered for. Not one of the broad-gauge locos was ever preserved, but Didcot Railway Centre has reconstructed an example, 2-2-2 *Fire Fly*.

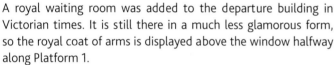

A royal waiting room was added to the departure building in Victorian times. It is still there in a much less glamorous form, so the royal coat of arms is displayed above the window halfway along Platform 1.

The crest of the GWR shows the cross and sword of London alongside the ship and castle of Bristol. It was of course Isambard Kingdom Brunel who linked these two cities in 1841 with his superbly engineered line.

When this line connected with Bristol, every town or city set its own time according to when the sun came up. The railway, with its direct connection, confused that. Hence this clock in Bristol has two minute hands, one eleven minutes apart from the other.

Castle Class 4-6-0 No. 7029 *Clun Castle* had the distinction of hauling a 'Farewell to Steam' special train service out of Paddington in November 1965. This made the loco a prime candidate for preservation. The class was the most successful express passenger locomotive in GWR history with 171 examples being built between 1923 and 1951. This example was outshopped by Swindon Works in 1950, therefore being one of the last. Here seen at the Tyseley Works in Birmingham, which maintains and runs this engine and many others including Castle Class No. 5043 *Earl of Mount Edgcumbe*, which is in the background.

One of the larger GWR 'Prairie' tank engines is seen here heading a suburban service from Paddington to Slough. These performed duties right through from the 1930s until steam finished for the Western Region in 1965. The 2-6-2T tanks had a high boiler pressure to enable them to have better acceleration and also cope with gradients such as those found in the nearby Westbourne Park underpass.

CHAPTER 12

BAKER STREET

Baker Street came into being in 1863 when the world's first underground railway opened between Farringdon and Paddington Station. The line was opened by the GWR to provide a link across London which would take its passengers eventually to Moorgate terminus in the City of London, the great world financial hub.

The line opened to suit the GWR's broad gauge track which was 7′ wide. A fulfilled ambition of Isambard Kingdom Brunel who wanted his railway to be the best and the most comfortable. However, all other railway companies disagreed and had their gauge at 5′ 8″ wide. This gauge become became a world standard and in the end Brunel, or rather his successors, succumbed and changed to the standard gauge in 1892. In the meantime, the line was equipped with a third rail to each track, giving it dual gauges.

With the tunnels having to accommodate broad gauge trains, they were built to a much more generous width and height than any tunnel solely built for standard gauge. Electrification didn't happen until 1906 so this generosity of width and height helped enormously to disperse the smoke from the locomotives.

Although the construction of these tunnels was performed by the cut-and-fill method, that at Baker Street was constructed using the traditional brick method. Light vents were added at intervals to both sides, which also let out smoke. This design gave the station a unique and distinctive appearance which can still be appreciated today. However, the light which now shines down is artificial.

The lines through to Paddington belonged to the Metropolitan Railway and, as with all the railway companies of those days, the Met had ambitions. Very soon after the line opened, the Met swung a branch off to take it to St John's Wood. Towards the end of the century the ambitions of the company had taken the railway out into the countryside of Middlesex and Buckinghamshire.

Edward Watkin, the supremo of the GCR which ran into Marylebone, had also become a director of the Met and chairman of the SER in Kent. Linking up his beloved Great Central with the Met and connecting at Baker Street, he could get through the tunnels to Farringdon and link up with the valuable river crossing at Blackfriars. However, by the 1890s, due to his failing health, his desire to extend right to the Continent fell flat.

The Met quadrupled its lines out to Harrow in 1900 which allowed for certain expansion which could be used by the Marylebone line. There were however different ambitions in the new century coming from the Metropolitan directors (who had built themselves a very smart headquarters building at Baker Street). All those acres of farmland in those rural counties of northwest London could be bought at agricultural prices. They could then make their own market of customers for their railway by becoming property developers. This they did with a vengeance, whereby they were very soon offering beautiful semis and detached properties with a bit of style and decorative timberwork to the front. They had inadvertently created a series of residential districts which became known as 'Metroland'. All within easy reach of a tidy little station which would bring the customers right along those ever expanding fast lines through to Baker Street and home again in the evening. It was all so easy.

To make this work successfully, Baker Street Station developed as a terminus. From there commuters could transfer to the Bakerloo Underground line, take the Circle line or a bus connection, as necessary.

The most famous resident of Baker Street is in fact fictitious. Sherlock Holmes was the private detective created by Sir Arthur Conan Doyle. Holmes, who lived at 221b Baker Street, is seen here without his sidekick, Watson, keeping an eye on his local station.

Every station liked to pay its respects to staff members who made the supreme sacrifice fighting for their country. Baker Street is no exception, but unlike some of the bigger stations, the names of the fallen fit onto one plate. Constructed in Carrara marble, a lion overcoming a serpent is at the top, while at the bottom it is noted that the memorial was erected by the directors, officers and staff of the railway.

Above: The slip road leads up from the main road with the Planetarium in the distance. The entrances lead through to platform level at the rear of the building. Three lines are available from here with the original cut-and-fill tracks being below Marylebone Road. A branch was taken off the original lines to connect the railway with the suburban area known as Metroland. The line of the Euston and Marylebone Roads defined the limit of where overground trains were originally allowed to run.

Opposite above: The huge building complex above Baker Street Station comprises railway offices, restaurants and high class flats. Finally completed in 1929 it was to be just four years after this that the Met was incorporated into Frank Pick's London Transport system. Later, signalling for the whole of the Met lines was operated from here. Looking across from Marylebone Road, the south facing frontage shows off the building at its best.

Opposite below: As with all Britain's trains, there is great nostalgia to keep the past alive. With the Metropolitan it is no different. Here at Chalfont and Latimer on the lines past Harrow on the Hill, the original Metropolitan No. 1 is doing steam duty. The class 0-4-4T engine was the last Metropolitan loco to be built at the Neasden works in 1898.

Above: A train for Aldgate slips away to join the 'first ever' Underground line running below the Marylebone and Euston Roads. The suburbs of north-west London connect to the City and Thameslink services via this very important link. Between Wembley Park and Baker Street there is a fast 'limited stop' service which gives residents living in the areas known as Metroland a fast run to and from work. Above the platform on the right the signs lead passengers to the deep-cut 'Tube' services of the Bakerloo and Jubilee lines.

Opposite above: The Chiltern Court flats and offices sit over the hollow of Baker Street Station. Therefore a massive structural support system has to be in place. This can be seen through the concourse areas of the station. It is always a little bit sad when there is no natural lighting to an area like this.

Opposite below: William H. Smith was there at the beginning, back in the 1840s. He was able to establish the newly-founded enterprise of selling newspapers on stations. (The papers expanded their enterprise with the rise of rail travel.) Here at Baker Street, Mr Smith would find his name still cast in stone, although this particular outlet was lost in the path of progress.

Left and below: Chiltern Court was built between 1911 and 1912.This was when the Metropolitan Railway became all-electric and extended services further through Middlesex and Buckinghamshire. With the railway not being seen from road level, the company added a few embellishments to let the public know it was there.

Right and below: Baker Street Station was one of the intermediate stations on the first ever underground railway in the world. That ran from Farringdon to Paddington and opened in 1863. The GWR broad-gauge tracks ran through before the narrower gauge became the standard. The station was built using the cut-and-fill method and the main road runs directly over the top. The change to the narrower tracks had the benefit of allowing the platforms to become wider. The vent-slots to the sides originally had a dual purpose – to let smoke out and to let light in. Now there is just natural lighting in those areas.

CHAPTER 13

LIVERPOOL STREET

Liverpool Street, in its present location, was a late arrival, with its terminus finally getting into town in 1875. The Great Eastern Railway (GER) had mopped up most of the smaller railway companies in East Anglia to finally bring its lines right into the heart of the City. The new station was at a below-ground level where the lines to the west side could connect with the Metropolitan Railway. The GER had its eyes on getting this connection which could give it access to Blackfriars and then the lines which ran to the south coast. The Met connection didn't prove successful and was finally closed off in 1907.

There was also a branch taken from the east side of the station where a connection could be made to curve to the right where Shoreditch station is now situated. This ran through Shadwell and onwards to cross below the Thames and join up with the Brighton lines from New Cross. For a very short time a Brighton timetabled service operated from Liverpool Street, but this proved short lived. The connection can still be seen 150 metres out of the station, although it is now partly bricked up.

Before Liverpool Street was reached, the GER had established a terminus, just across from Bethnal Green Station and later on a high-level site north of the present station, called Bishopsgate (although this was in Shoreditch). It proved to be an unfortunate location, for it was not convenient for the City and was built adjoining one of the worst slum areas in the East End. Once built it displaced hundreds of families who then made the area even more overcrowded. By this time in the century, the government had legislated to the effect that a railway company had to rehouse displaced families affected by massive railway development. Various slum clearance developments were therefore built in the area.

Liverpool Street was always 'uncomfortable'. With the longer lines splitting the station in half, access had to be provided by the high-level walkway. Three generations never saw the building in its non-blackened state, therefore there was great apathy about it. One of the busiest stations it might have been, but one of the most popular it was not.

In 1975 all that was about to change, for British Rail (BR) had decided to develop the site and sell as much space as it could for offices. A first scheme in 1973 would have wiped out the old station completely, taking with it all the Victorian ironwork. Fortunately that scheme found its way into the bin, and led to BR getting better advice. The design team, led by Nick Derbyshire with his assistant Alistair Lansley, came up with a solution which was actually going to make the station liked again. Yes, a huge amount of office space could be built, but cleverly some new sections of ironwork could be added to a good amount of that already there.

Broad Street Station, which was adjacent to Liverpool Street, had already been shown its end and was redeveloped under the 'Broadgate Scheme'. But that was separate. Careful planning, demolition and reconstruction was undertaken to the main station of Liverpool Street, bringing it all into one area – which was below the Victorian ironwork, built to match. The east side of the station together with its 1890s roof were sacrificed. The roof had been in the ordinary 'ridge and furrow' style, so it was not missed. The whole of the east side was then redeveloped, keeping the platforms below. Also, a new development was added crossways, at the north end of the platforms. Unfortunately this removed the former open area at the throat of the station, but the sacrifice was worth it for what we have been left with. The hotel and offices together with all other remaining buildings were upgraded. The platforms and station concourse were remodelled with a grand new roof over the concourse. All was well done and appreciated.

Opposite: The new twin towers (built 1991) front onto Liverpool Street. The section of roof nicely leads in to join with the beautifully extended internal roof of similar appearance. The station was built in a dip which had a ramped roadway going down at this point before the reorganisations of the 1990s removed this. The steps are up to the walkway level inside the station where passengers can descend or take advantage of the little coffee shops. The offices on the left are in place of the former Broad Street Station, which was demolished in 1986.

Above: The station offices seen in the yellow brickwork served as the headquarters of the GER. Beyond the offices and fronting onto Liverpool Street is the original hotel, of course called the Great Eastern. This opened a decade after the station in 1885 with the larger section coming along twenty years after that. The taxis emerged through the hotel from the station at the end of the first section. Now they are using just the street. The yellow brick offices were completely rebuilt to suit modern standards in the 1990s but the outside appearance was retained.

Opposite above: Postcard showing Broad Street Station which adjoined Liverpool Street until its closure and demolition in 1986. That station was at high level as against Liverpool Street Station being built at sub-ground level. The lines of each never met, with Broad Street services having connections to the North London Line at Dalston Junction.

Opposite below: The corner of Bishopsgate and Liverpool Street, where this impressive station hotel stands. All these major stations needed their hotel, especially here because for a long time this was the only one in the City of London. The part in Liverpool Street (to the left) was built first, opening in 1884, with the stylish extension onto Bishopsgate coming at the turn of the century. The architect was the same man who designed the Marylebone Hotel.

Above: Part of the late 1980s to early 90s development. The entrance onto Bishopsgate leads down to the new concourse. With the hotel on the left the office building on the right covers the eastern side of the station, Platforms 13 to 18.

Opposite above: A view of the restyled interior dating from the improvements of the early 1990s. All the ironwork and glazing seen in this picture is new. For the convenience of modern construction it is all constructed in steel. This is part of the thoughtful planning which this station benefited from in the mid-1980s when BR's architecture and design department got just about everything right. It is a scheme which has combined the best of the past with the best of the new. In the very early days of this station two sets of rail lines would pass across this space to provide a goods collecting area below the hotel. A cab road would cross here too. Because of that, the station always needed a good selection of high-level walkways.

Opposite below: Another view from walkway level with a glimpse down the station. The new steel structure connects with the old wrought iron roof structures halfway along the station.

Above: The Norwich train has arrived. The last, and soon to be obsolete, main line service still powered by a dedicated locomotive. At the front is the 900 Class electric loco which will also power the train in the reverse direction. Modern trains get replaced with very little fanfare.

Opposite above: The west side of the station with all the new steelwork still glistening. This side takes the trains which veer of northwards at Bethnal Green to the suburbs of north-east London. The station is still famous for the intense service which operated from these platforms after World War I and into the next decades. The N7 tank engines of the day operated a ten-minute turnround at peak times to look after the people the station was put here to serve. After all, the construction did displace thousands of people, many of whom were rehoused near Bethnal Green.

Opposite below: Once upon a time the rail throat at the end of the station was open to the elements. Not any more! The planning of the new station, which began in the 1970s, instantly saw that the space above those railway lines was potentially prime for top-dollar office footage. The picture confirms that the potential was attained and delivered the funds for the expansion of the lovely arches. They got it right. The trains pass into the dark undercroft before emerging to make the 1 in 70 climb to Bethnal Green.

Above: Connoisseurs of railway architecture do like a good deal of natural light to come upon their station. And here we see that situation in top order. No, the old glass at the other end didn't get replaced, but nobody looks at that anyway. The lovely new glazing is clear and sparkling and always will be. The structure consists of two aisles with two naves separated by a double line of support columns down the middle. All replaced in the 1986–1991 rebuilding.

Opposite above: A heart-warming bronze statue stands at the street entrance to the station. It is by Frank Meisler and Arie Oviada and depicts the arrival from Germany in 1938 and 1939 of about 10,000 unaccompanied Jewish children, who were transported to Britain to escape the persecution in Germany and Austria. These children, who were never likely to see their families again, arrived at Liverpool Street Station to be taken in by local families and foster homes. The statue serves also as a reminder of the London children who were evacuated from this station in the autumn of 1939.

Opposite below: The intense timetables of the suburban services from here in the 1920s are legendary. It should not be forgotten that later decades also responded to the need to serve the ever increasing number of commuters. In the 1970s, middle-distance trains left from both Platforms 12 and 13 (seen here) at ten-minute intervals in the evening rush hour.

Liverpool Street - 1

A survivor from the Jazz Service days, this Class N7 tank engine is the only example of the fleet which admirably performed the intensive service to areas of north-east London. More powerful smaller engines had come in to pull the ever increasingly heavy suburban services. No. 69621 (which is a post-1948 number) is still doing its job superbly in preservation. Here seen on the North Norfolk Railway.

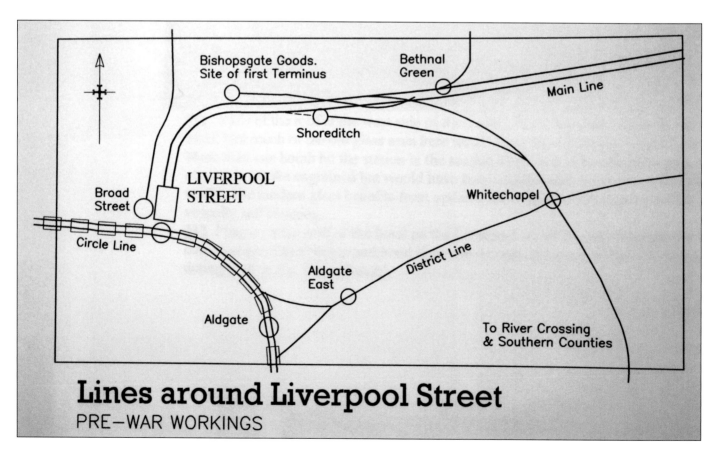

Lines around Liverpool Street
PRE—WAR WORKINGS

Section of map which shows the railway arrangements in the early part of the twentieth century. The main point of interest is the location of the Bishopsgate goods depot which, before 1874, was the GER terminus. The bend out of Liverpool Street arrives at Bishopsgate Junction where a southbound connection was made through Shoreditch and Whitechapel to destinations south of the River Thames.

Above and right: The far end of the station where the lines came into the open was always going to be targeted for development. Especially between 1986 and 2004, as much space as practicable was sold off to pay for the station upgrading. However, the former throat end could now get a place in any book about 'Secret London'. For it has an open area available to all, equivalent to the London 'squares'. The area is called Exchange Square – surrounded on three sides by office blocks and on the other by the end of the 1874 train shed. Unseen and below is still where the trains run. It is another compliment to the planners in getting considerable daylight into what is now the 'murky' end of the station. Office workers on their lunchtime break are even able to watch a big screen where the second day of a Lord's Ashes Test match is on view. The date is August 2019.

The former taxi road which ran the length of the station. Here it emerged, for the cabs to leave the station having dropped down from the bridge at the far end. The northern entry is still there and used by goods vehicles to this day. Vehicles can turn to use the one entry/exit point in the road behind the building between Platforms 10 and 13. With the station being at the lower level, cabs would emerge at this end after making the easy climb from concourse level. The plaque on the wall depicts the former use of this site as the Bethlehem Hospital.

No railway company could resist having its name or initials carved in masonry or cast iron sections – as many times as possible. For this station it is the GER, seen here high up on the hotel.

Back of the hotel with the roof butting up. The arch is the former cab and goods vehicle exit point. This is opposite Platforms 10–13 where, in the early days, trains crossed the concourse for goods trains to discharge their loads below the hotel. Because of this and also because the station was below street level, passenger flow relied on a system of walkways to circulate to all platforms.

Looking across the concourse from the hotel walkway, the new sections of glazed roofing catch the eye in a very pleasing way. This western side of the station didn't formerly have the iron structure coming back this far. There was solid building infill at this point. It is commendable that the BR designers overcame pressure to do something else and extended the lines and roofing back to this point. The walkway with little tea rooms etc. is a tribute to the old station concept which had the same thing but obviously in its old form.

Aerial view of Liverpool Street Station in the 1950s. The elevated Broad Street Station is on the left.

Above left: One of the new columns near the front of the station with acanthus leaf decoration applied to the capital. This decoration was also applied to original columns where it had been removed. The rivets tell us that the archwork is of steel construction.

Above right: At the back of the station, the old columns and arches are still there, as are the original rivets. The floral capital decorations and trims have been restored to all original columns. It is usual for all valley gutters to stations to discharge rainwater into pipes running inside columns. Here the plastic rainwater pipes would discharge into cast- or light-iron pipes within the columns.

Right: With the demolition of the former Broad Street Station, the site has now received its second reconstruction. The declining use of the station was always going to lead to its removal. This and Holborn Viaduct station are actually the only major London terminus stations to be lost completely. London office space is so valuable that everything has to be very successful to survive. Broad Street's route northward has now been picked up from nearby Shoreditch Station where the lines run through to connect with other services covering East and south-east London.

When steam finished in the mid-1960s two classes of diesel locomotive took over the main line duties for services to Norwich, the 37s and the 47s. A Class 47 is here in the distance with a Class 37 in the foreground. Behind the 37 is a suburban stalwart – a Class 31.

View of the roof at the west side of the station. It is very clear where the new and old meet. Not much of the old glass seen here would have been from the original station of 1874. More than one bomb hit the station in World War II. The old glass seen is still obviously smoke engrained but would have been cleaned and renovated at the time of the new works. The modern glass benefits from modern construction techniques which leave it virtually self-cleaning.

The plaque on the wall of the hotel on the Liverpool Street elevation speaks for itself. In the construction of this station and hotel there are records of large numbers of skeletons found dating back to the Black Death.

THE CORPORATION OF

SITE OF THE FIRST BETHLEHEM HOSPITAL 1247 – 1676

THE CITY OF LONDON

A selection of 'B' Class engines wait outside Liverpool Street. The date is April 1948, just four months after the railways were nationalised. The LNER had become the Eastern Region.

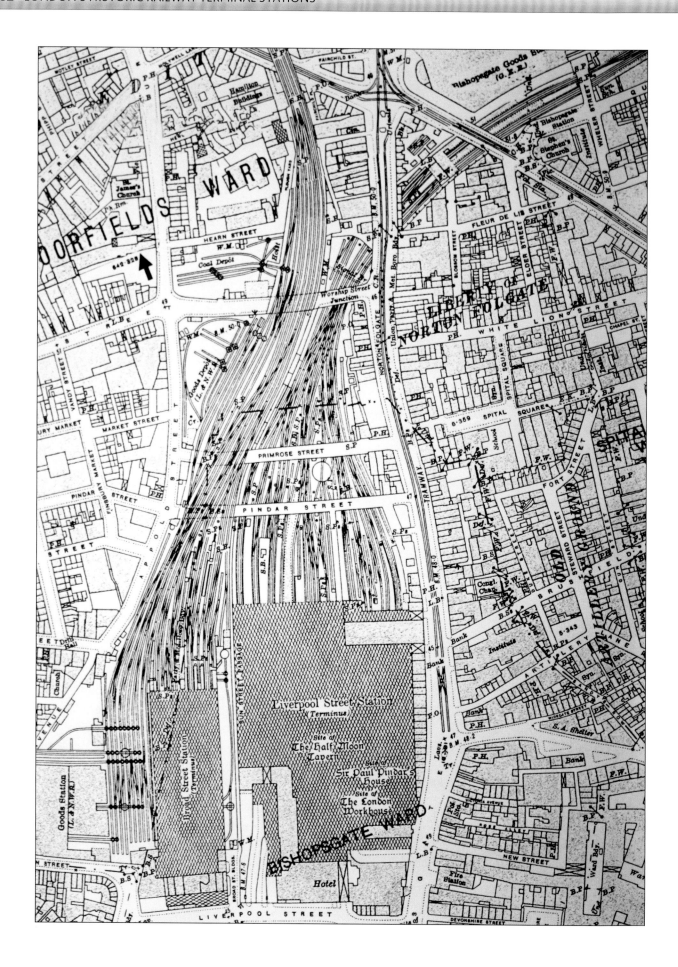

Above: A Britannia Class loco gets up steam to head a mid- or long-range service. This was the flagship of the standard classes promoted by the government after nationalisation, many being allocated to this station. Note the Gresley teak-bodied bow-ended parcels van.

Opposite: A mid-century map showing the Liverpool Street layout with surrounding roads. The site of Bishopsgate Goods Depot (near the top) is where the station was originally sited before it came down to the present site. Note the tramlines in Bishopsgate. These stop just short of the City of London boundary, for no tram was allowed to cross that hallowed border.

CHAPTER 14

FENCHURCH STREET & DOCKLANDS LIGHT

In 1841 the little London & Blackwall Railway (L&BR) became the first to penetrate the hallowed Roman walls of the City of London (the 'London Wall'). The L&BR first extended a line westward towards the capital, stopping at The Minories, a couple of hundred metres short of its final resting place. The difficulties were such that the trains had to be cable-hauled for the whole three and a half miles. They were aiming for the City as they had made their base close to the East and West India docks. As was usual when constructing a railway through a built-up area, the structure was carried on brick arches.

So great a prize was it to get a line this far that the L&BR soon had all the bigger companies wanting some of the action. The London & Birmingham Railway (L&B) had built a line across the boroughs of North London and had eyes on connecting to the docks for the movement of goods traffic. The L&B also liked the idea of getting into the City of London. By 1850 it had made a connection and three years later had changed its name to the North London Railway (NLR).

The L&BR had forseen this by taking a branch to stop just short of the Eastern Counties line to Stratford, where a station was placed without a connection being made. The L&B had also reached Stratford and soon connected with the new partner, now not only getting to the docks but able to provide a passenger service from Islington to Fenchurch Street.

The two companies now jointly used Fenchurch Street with the station being rebuilt by the L&B to what we have today. The first extension into Fenchurch Street resulted in the construction of a two-storey structure with an overall timber roof. In 1854 the bigger station was completed.

The L&B stayed for a decade or two before getting its own terminus at Broad Street, next to Liverpool Street Station. It had always been in the L&BR's interest to attract other railways, which gave it good finance. The company to expand in what was still the 'railway mania'

days. Knocking on the door was the company which was geographically suited to take over the southern Essex services, the London, Tilbury & Southend Railway (LTSR).

The Fenchurch Street line was really only suited to serve southern Essex along the corridor which follows the Thames to the estuary. Paddle steamers plied the Thames to the burgeoning resort of Southend, which was to give the railway its best business for the next century. The coming of the railways had lifted little coastal towns like Southend to the status of major resorts. Southend became the playground for East Londoners who couldn't get enough of visits to the Kurzal funfair and walks along the mile and a quarter pleasure pier. Liverpool Street also opened a separate line to Southend via Shenfield.

Thomas Cook had begun the idea of running excursion trains for the Temperance Movement in Leicester. The idea was quickly picked up by every railway company who could offer a cheap day-return to allow families to travel to a special location. Fenchurch Street quickly offered day excursion outings for families to Southend, something which was still being offered a century later. The author's father took the family on one of these excursions in the 1950s and we waited with great delight to experience the rides of the Kurzal funfair. The fare for the return trip was 3/6d for an adult (17p) and the use of first class accommodation was permitted.

No other railway had got so close to the Bank of England area of the city as the LTSR, which led the major players from the North wanting to get to Fenchurch Street. The mighty MR and GNR were both to achieve some success in fulfilling these ambitions.

Amazingly, in 1912, the MR absorbed the LTSR, promising electrification – a claim which couldn't be fulfilled owing to the coming of war. But another twist took place in 1923 when the government gave Fenchurch Street to the LNER (which had absorbed the GNR). Nothing more could have upset the Midland, now part of the LMS, but the Tilbury/Southend line still was attributable to them. Both had long since had access to the docks, which was their greatest prize.

A new market had grown over the years which was to put huge pressure on the tracks into the station: the growth of commuter traffic and the expansion of towns and villages all across the catchment area. A Tilbury cut-off line had been installed to make the journey to Southend six miles shorter. This later led to the emergence of a new town appearing, called Basildon. Such pressure and overcrowding soon led to the nickname of 'Misery Line' being applied by the entrenched customers.

Electrification of services was not to happen until after nationalisation in 1948, and steam was still to be the prime power source until 1961. Prior to that occurred one of the best steam 'swansongs' in the country. Electrification wasn't to come to the line until the late 1950s – ten years after the Liverpool Street line was electrified. Steam had battled on with engines being overworked and under-serviced. To haul the heavy trains, the large tank engines with the 2-6-4T wheel arrangement had been utilised for the former LTSR London, Southend and Shoeburyness route. Many engine designers had produced a version of this powerful locomotive, with the Stanier LMS version from 1935 being one of them. An LMS Fairburn version had also been represented, but with masses of bad publicity being thrown at the railway for breakdowns and cancellations, in 1958 several of the Riddles Standard Class 4 were added to the fleet. Suddenly, with an end-of-steam date in sight, the tide of thought turned in favour of these powerful brutes. Upkeep was good and they all gave a final show of what they could do. Out they went with all the enthusiasts saddened to see them replaced by the very clean and efficient electric trains.

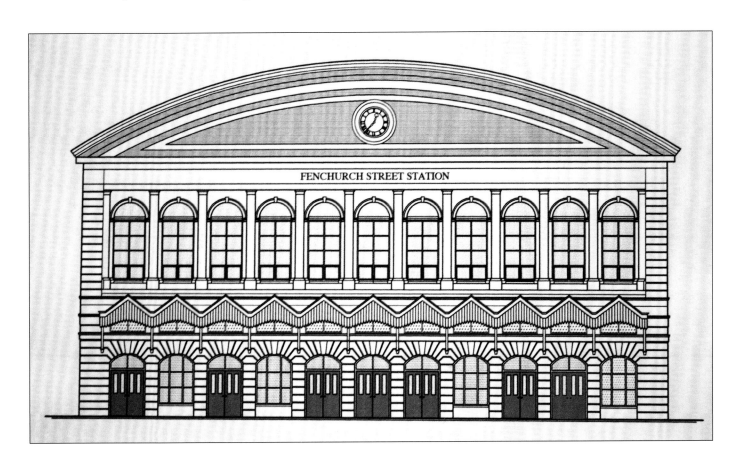

The lines to Loughton and Ongar were laid when the green fields of those places were fancied for middle-class dwellings. The connections to the City were just right for the monied set. All the railways of the North and East wanted to connect with what the L&B had, which was connections to docklands and the City. They all did, especially after the Grouping of 1923 when both the LNER and LMS had different controlling and running powers. With the variety of destinations available from this station, it became normal for wooden destination boards to be fitted to the front of locomotives. Note the high stovepipe chimney to give better draught to the fire.

Fenchurch Street station in its present form, as seen from the front, dates from 1854. A rebuilding took place at that time to supersede a timber structure which was constructed when the L&BR expanded from its previous end location. That was at Minories, just a short distance, but it penetrated into the hallowed City of London. The arch shape of the roof seen here matched the outline of the iron and glass roof beyond. Now sadly no longer: the lure of income from office space tempted BR in the 1980s.

A view eastwards from the end of the platforms shows, on the right, the London terminus station of the Docklands Light Railway (DLR). Also the parapet over the road called Minories. The first station here would have been sited where the electric train now is. The small four-wheel carriages were firstly pushed into the new station by hand from a cable-haul system. This view in 1845 would have been incredible.

The office development (with garden) sits over the station. Long gone is the iron and glass arched roof. At the platform is c2c 357006, a class which came to this station in 2002. In November 2018, the station operators realised that this was a significant date and adorned the trains with poppies and the words *Remembering Our Fallen 88 1914–1918*. It was the hundredth anniversary of the end of that war.

Before the nationalisation of the railways in 1948 the LMS had running powers over the LTSR. In 1934 it took the chance to add Stanier tank engine 2-6-4T three-cylinder No. 2500 to the fleet, where it spent all its working life until the withdrawal of steam in 1961. Another similar class on the line at that time was the Fairburn two-cylinder 2-6-4T type. This style of large tank engine perpetuated through different companies since Fowler's introduction in 1927 of a two-cylindered type.

Steam on the London, Basildon, Southend and Shoeburyness line enjoyed a great finale in 1961 which was warmly embraced by enthusiasts. Documentary films were also made. Great steam it was, but misery for the City passengers in the old stock of the railway. The British Standard Class large tank 2-6-4T 2-cylinder No. 80072 was on the railway joining the former Stanier and Fairburn tanks of the same style. They and their fellow engines fought it out with spirit, probably to try and see which was the best performer. No. 80072, seen here at Tenterden in Kent, appeared in all those documentary films.

Steam engines began to work from Fenchurch Street from 1849. The most successful in that century were the Terriers. They were good enough to survive almost until the end of steam and eight survive in preservation, including No. 672 0-6-0T *Fenchurch*. Terriers were a class which worked suburban traffic until larger engines were required as demand grew. No. 672 is now on the Bluebell Railway.

Just a few paces from Fenchurch Street Station, Tower Gateway opened in 1987 as the London terminus of the DLR. Very successfully it links the capital to the new financial centre on the Isle of Dogs/Canary Wharf. It also connects to Stratford for main line and other interchanges. There is also a branch going south of the Thames to Greenwich, Woolwich and Lewisham. The road is the Minories – the boundary of the City of London.

Above: The drivers-eye view from the DLR train as it closes in on Tower Gateway Station. However, these trains do not have drivers – all are controlled from a central office. Here there is just a single DLR line going into the station, where the trains have use of platforms on both sides. Alongside is a disused DLR connection which connects to the City spur, with the Fenchurch Street platforms being visible on the right.

Opposite above: A DLR train has arrived at Stratford. Here a dedicated terminus platform is located opposite the Olympic Park. The railway has a policy of minimal staffing and that includes on the train. The main line tracks into Liverpool Street are on the right.

Opposite below: Many lines are sharing the raised former Tilbury and Southend routes into the capital. On the left are the tracks of the DLR descending to make an extension right into the heart of the City of London. However, this at present is unused. The Fenchurch Street lines are on the far right.

CHAPTER 15

MOORGATE & FARRINGDON

In one respect Farringdon Station has become a very important one in the capital. For now it stands as the crossroads for north/south trains running through London. It was also the first Underground terminus station in London. It was from here that the first subground line was opened, anywhere in the world, in 1863.

In the Baker Street chapter more is said about the line's origin, which was constructed using the cut-and-fill method. Both the Euston and Marylebone Roads were closed and then excavated to form a brick-lined trench. The lines were then laid and the roof added. The roof was of course topped by the road surfaces. Tunnels branching off the new lines were made at King's Cross, St Pancras and Baker Street, and the line went on to terminate on the west side of Paddington Station.

This construction work caused massive disruption, for all the traffic had to be diverted and adjoining buildings propped. But the wait and trouble was worthwhile, for the first part of the London Underground system had been put in place. Farringdon was on the edge of the City of London, but a couple of years later, in 1865, an extension was made to Moorgate. This then became the terminus for the Metropolitan Railway.

All services were steam hauled, and were offered through the branches at King's Cross and St Pancras to outlying towns north of London such Hertford and Bedford. A new below-ground connection was opened in 1904 between Moorgate and Finsbury Park to avoid those notorious connections at King's Cross.

Southward from Farringdon, in 1866, the southbound connection to Blackfriars Station (which was south of the river) had been made and a branch from Blackfriars connected with Moorgate. This, then, was the most sought-after stretch of railway in the capital, as it made the connection from north to south available to everyone. And all those companies wanted it. As the decades wore on, the cross-river services became less popular with passengers. One of the reasons was a terrible 1 in 39 climb through a tunnel from Farringdon Station to the bridge over Ludgate Hill. Virtually all trains had to have a banking engine connected to the back to make this horrible climb. From below ground level at Farringdon to the viaduct level of the river crossing was a health check

at the best of times. A passenger service like this couldn't survive but for goods trains it remained invaluable.

The government sponsored improvements of the line, called Thameslink, and resurrected this north/south service for passengers. The bridge over Ludgate Hill was removed in 1991 and the line was rebuilt in a new tunnel connecting to the new and improved Blackfriars Station. Long gone are the steam engines and we are left with clean and comfortable rail services for everyone. The improvements had their final implementation between 2010 and 2016 and it is all there for us to admire and use today.

The southern electric trains cross the river to go as far as Farringdon with their third rail pick-up system. They then raise their overhead antennas to connect with the north of London overhead system to take their services onward. Now it is possible to travel from somewhere like Bedford to Brighton. The new Crossrail services have given a boost to both Moorgate and Farringdon stations which provide part of the east/west route. For the first time Moorgate will connect with Liverpool Street, with a new booking hall to the east side of Moorgate and the west side of Liverpool Street station providing the link.

The Metropolitan Railway was always independent of other lines and remained that way until 1933. Then, after having a life on its own for seventy years, it was coerced into becoming part of the newly formed London Transport. On Moorgate Station is an example of the Met's last logo – obviously giving inspiration to the original bar and red disc the underground system came in with. These days Moorgate has lost out as being a terminus station.

Moorgate is connected to its near neighbour at Liverpool Street below ground, but only has two small access points at road level. With the station losing its everyday terminus activity, it now uses just two platforms serving the through trains of the Metropolitan, Circle and Hammersmith lines.

This 1865 print shows early morning workers dispersing from their train at Moorgate. They would be using a newly built extension from the Farringdon line where the first underground railway in the world came in from Paddington – this was in 1863. The government made it conditional that when a new Act for a railway was passed for London travel, cheap early morning fares should be made available for workers. This also helped these people move away from Central London to better accommodation a little further out. These cheap fares lasted until after World War II.

Above: These electrically powered locomotives were introduced in 1923 largely to take trains onwards from Baker Street to the outer reaches of the Metropolitan Railway. They could also serve trains to the City at Moorgate in rush hours. Here the only survivor of a fleet of twenty *Sarah Siddons*, comes back to visit Moorgate.

Left: The bus service from Shepherd's Bush to Liverpool Street shows a torturous route which must have taken a couple of hours to complete. Especially as it stopped at three terminus stations on the way. Top deck passengers look to be a bit exposed as would be the driver. The headlights are in an interesting place.

Opposite: This aerial shot taken after the ravages of war shows how open the station was. Also the number of platforms indicates the station's importance as a terminus. Now, of course, everything is underground. Only the two right-hand tracks are still used – as a through station. Two others have been kept, generally for carriage storage. The others have gone, as has the space above – all to offices.

Above: The turning of part of Cowcross Street into a pedestrian zone enabled Thameslink to have its own entrance and concourse. The government-sponsored upgrading of stations for Thameslink enabled the platforms here to be extended and they can now accommodate twelve-carriage trains. The extended platforms run past the entrance shown here. With the addition of Crossrail, this station now has the only central London interchange providing north-south and east-west main line through-routes. Farringdon station sits just outside the City of London, and is well situated to serve many areas.

Opposite above: A typical view of an open platform at Moorgate at the turn of the century. In the background is a huge retaining wall with every bit of space on it sold for advertising.

Opposite below: LMS Fowler 3MT 2-6-2 tank prepares to take a service away from Moorgate terminus. The date is May 1960 with the 6.30pm train about to head for Farringdon and pass through the widened lines (from the GWR broad gauge days) of the Metropolitan Railway tunnels to connect with the suburban lines out of St Pancras.

Above: The division of the station is clear to see: an interchange between two independent operators of the network. Crossing both of these lines at a much lower level is the new Crossrail service with its station between Farringdon and Barbican stations. With an easy connection, the station will again have a higher status. Its previous upgrading came in 2018 when Thameslink came fully on line.

Opposite above: Looking here in a south-easterly direction, the Met lines veer to their easterly route, while the Thameslink services follow right to take the southerly route which crosses the river at Blackfriars. It is at this station that the southbound trains change to the third rail pick-up.

Opposite below: With the road level visible on the right, it becomes clear to see how the cut-and-fill construction method worked. Here at the station there is double width, but further on the lines take up the space of one road. Looking towards the westbound direction, the Thameslink lines on the left will fall and then turn northwards to destinations north of London. On the right are the tracks of the Metropolitan and Circle lines.

Sarah Siddons arrives at Farringdon but with the wrong destination board. She has just come from Moorgate, and is not going there. This is a special running to commemorate the 150th anniversary of the opening of the Farringdon to Paddington Underground. On the rear of this train is the Metropolitan steam loco No. 1.

Always a busy station, the interchange works well. This view from the road bridge clearly shows the ending of the Southern third-rail electrical running system. From here northwards, the driver raises a pantograph above his train to connect to the overhead wires which are used in all the main line systems going northwards. The train in the station is an experimental 700 Class which uses both systems. The train will be running from Bedford or Peterborough to destinations south including Brighton. After crossing the river all services then call at London Bridge before continuing onwards.

LMS Fowler 2-6-2 No. 40026 ex-Moorgate large tank engine at Farringdon preparing to take a service through the Metropolitan tunnels. Fowler designed this style of more powerful tank engine in the early 1930s. So popular were they that the style was then copied and adapted by other chief mechanical engineers such as Stanier, Gresley, Fairburn etc. Variations were also added to the range of British Standard types introduced by BR from the early 1950s. The train sits on the lines coming from the Thames crossing at a time when no passenger trains took that route – hence before the lines had electrification. The date is 13 May 1960.

St. Pancras Station

Pre Eurostar - Section at 1980 timezone.

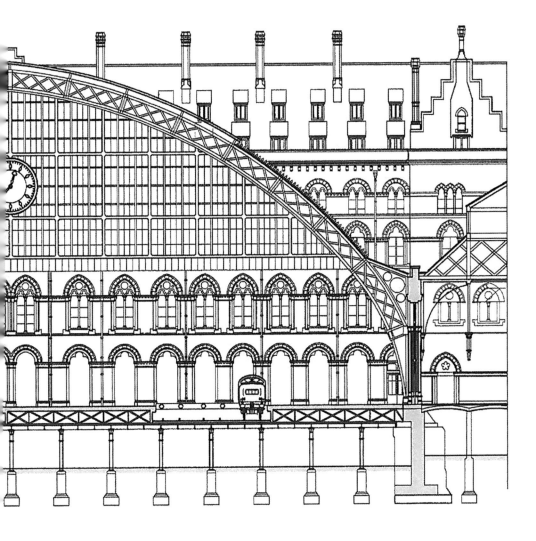

ABBREVIATIONS

BR	British Railways		LC&DR	London Chatham and Dover Railway
DLR	Docklands Light Railway		LGR	London and Greenwich Railway
GCR	Great Central Railway		LMS	London Midland and Scottish Railway
GER	Great Eastern Railway		LNER	London and North Eastern Railway
GNR	Great Northern Railway		LNWR	London & North Western Railway
GWR	Great Western Railway		LTSR	London, Tilbury & Southend Railway
L&B	London & Birmingham Railway		MR	Midland Railway
L&BR	London & Blackwall Railway		MS&LR	Manchester, Sheffield & Lincolnshire Railway
L&CR	London & Croydon Railway			
L&SWR	London & South Western Railway		SER	South Eastern Railway
LB&SCR	London Brighton and South Coast Railway		SE&CR	South Eastern & Chatham Railway
			SR	Southern Railway

ACKNOWLEDGEMENTS

230 photographs by the Author.

John Scott-Morgan Collection. 21b, 45b, 66b, 67t, 67b, 81b, 82, 83t, 98b, 115t, 115b, 196t.

The Transport Treasury supply. 46, 100, 155b, 181b, 183, 196b, 201.

Photographer not known. 20b, 180t.

CAD Drawings and maps by Author.

Other prints and B&W photographs from Author's collection including postcards.

The Author would like to give sincere thanks to Janet Brookes and her colleagues of P&S for constructing this book under difficult conditions.

INDEX